Children, Families and Schools

Effective communication between the home and school is crucial for any child's education, but where special educational needs are concerned, creating good partnerships is essential. This book is concerned with home–school relations from an 'inclusive' perspective. Throughout, it highlights issues that are common across all children and families, those that reflect individual diversity and those that are of particular significance when children have special educational needs.

Sally Beveridge provides debate on issues such as:

- the conceptual and policy frameworks that form the background to this subject;
- the fundamental nature of the learning environment that families represent for children;
- the potential role of home–school relations in supporting the educational achievements of children from diverse backgrounds and with differing needs;
- strategies for the development of positive communication with parents.

This book offers a clear and coherent overview of a complex topic, ensuring its appeal to students and practitioners alike.

Sally Beveridge is Senior Lecturer in Education at the University of Leeds.

Children, Families and Schools

Developing partnerships for inclusive education

Sally Beveridge

RoutledgeFalmer
Taylor & Francis Group

LONDON AND NEW YORK

First published 2005 by RoutledgeFalmer
2 Park Square, Milton Park, Abingdon, Oxon OX14 4RN

Simultaneously published in the USA and Canada
by RoutledgeFalmer
270 Madison Ave, New York NY 10016

RoutledgeFalmer is an imprint of the Taylor & Francis Group

Typeset in Times and Gill by BC Typesetting Ltd, Bristol
Printed and bound in Great Britain by
TJ International Ltd, Padstow, Cornwall

British Library Cataloguing in Publication Data
A catalogue record for this book is available from the British Library

Library of Congress Cataloging in Publication Data
A catalog record for this book has been requested

ISBN 0–415–27933–X (hbk)
ISBN 0–415–27934–8 (pbk)

Contents

Illustrations

Figures

Boxes

Acknowledgements

I am grateful for the contribution that so many parents, teachers and colleagues have made over the years to the development of the ideas presented in this book. Special thanks are due to Patrick Wiegand for the insights and support offered throughout the writing process.

Chapter 1

Introduction

This book is concerned with children, families and schools. Its main themes centre on the nature of home–school relationships and the impact of these on children's development and learning. Within the context of the home–school relationship, it seeks to highlight the importance of recognising the role of children as active participants in educational processes. Throughout, links are also made to the development of inclusive educational practice, and particular attention is given to issues relating to children with special educational needs. This chapter provides a brief introduction to the themes and their interrelationships.

Home–school relationships

It has long been recognised that the quality of home–school relationships is associated with the educational outcomes that children achieve. In this country, official recognition of the significance of home–school relationships dates as far back as the Plowden Report on primary education (DES, 1967), which described partnership between parents and teachers as 'one of the essentials' for promoting children's educational achievements. Almost all government reports since then have endorsed the general principle that the closer and more positive the communication and collaboration between their teachers and parents, the better the outcomes for children.[1] This principle is supported by the steady accumulation of research evidence that has built up over the years to demonstrate an association at an individual level between parental involvement and children's academic attainments (e.g. Hewison and Tizard, 1980; Coleman, 1998), and at a whole school level, between parent–teacher relationships, school effectiveness and school improvement (e.g. Ball, 1998;

Wolfendale and Bastiani, 2000). More recently, positive home–school relationships have also been linked to the promotion of inclusive educational practice (e.g. Gartner and Lipsky, 1999; Mittler, 2000).

Within educational policy, the terms 'partnership with parents' and 'home–school partnership' have become well-established ways of referring to the ideal relationship that is aimed for. Although the terms are used in different ways and with differing emphases, there has been an increasing consensus that the notion of partnership must be underpinned by a recognition and valuing of the complementary roles that parents and teachers play in children's education. This notion is not unproblematic, however, for despite the implicit principle of equality that it conveys, in practice parents rarely perceive that they have equal status to professionals in educational decision-making (Armstrong, 1995). Further, it is evident that the nature of home–school relationships is affected by gender, ethnicity and social class variables (Vincent, 1996). Accordingly, while there is little doubt that children benefit when home–school communication is characterised by reciprocity, trust and respect, it is important to acknowledge the diversity of relationships that exist between parents and teachers, and to recognise how distant these can be from the partnership ideal.

The quality of home–school relationships is influenced by a large range of interacting factors. Within school, it is evident that teachers vary in the attitudes, knowledge, understanding, skills and commitment that they bring to their interactions with parents. Schools and Local Education Authorities (LEAs) also vary in both their policies and the degree of support they provide for this aspect of the teaching role. Similarly parents differ, for example in their confidence in dealing with the authority that schools represent, and in their familiarity with and expectations for their children's formal education. Practical barriers to easy communication with schools can also arise, such as transport arrangements, or domestic and work commitments. Crucially, the home–school relationship is also influenced by the child himself or herself. It is apparent, for example, that where parents see that their children are liked and valued by teachers, they are more likely to feel positive about communication and cooperation with school. At the same time, however, there is evidence that children seek to preserve some privacy in their home and school lives and to 'manage the gap' (Alldred et al., 2002) between them.

If schools are to develop their interaction with parents in line with partnership ideals, it is essential to acknowledge the complex nature of this three-way relationship between parent, teacher and child, and the ways in which this evolves over time as the child grows older. It is argued in this book, therefore, that partnerships between teachers and parents must also promote the role of children as active participants in their own education.

The active participation of children in educational processes

Research into children's lives outside school (e.g. Brannen and O'Brien, 1996; James *et al.*, 1999) has contributed to a recognition that children are not simply recipients of socialisation processes such as those initiated by their parents and teachers, but are active social agents in their own right, who both contribute to and hold their own distinct views on their experiences. With this shifting perception of childhood has come an increasing acknowledgement that child and parent or pupil and teacher perspectives do not necessarily coincide, and further, that children have the right to express their views and be listened to in matters that concern them.

By comparison with parent partnership, the principle of pupil participation in decision-making is not yet very well-established in educational policy. Nevertheless, within the school context, there is growing evidence that children do better personally, socially and academically when they are encouraged to take responsibility for their own learning (e.g. Cox, 2000; Weare, 2000; Bearne, 2002). Accordingly, greater attention is now being paid to ways of promoting their active involvement in educational processes. The notion of pupil participation, like the idea of parent partnership, is complex. It involves questions of power and responsibility as well as the need to accommodate diverse professional and community priorities and perspectives. It is apparent, for example, that principles of participation do not always fit comfortably with either a teacher's professional stance or with a family's cultural values. What is more, as a number of authors have begun to note (e.g. Brannen *et al.*, 2000; Wyness, 2000), there is a potential tension between the principle of pupil participation and that of parent partnership. These writers observe that, if parents and teachers develop close communication and collaboration, then there is a risk that schools come to regard parents as always speaking for their children, rather than acknowledging that parents and children may hold differing perspectives. Where this is the case, the involvement of parents can serve to reduce the developing autonomy of their children in decision-making.

While these are real concerns, the risk must surely be reduced if both parents and teachers are alert to the need to listen to and take account of children's views. What is required is an explicit attempt to develop the home–school partnership in ways which support rather than constrain children's active involvement. Indeed, there is scope for potential two-way support between parents and teachers when it comes to promoting children's participation in decision-making both in and out of school (Beveridge, 2004). Parents typically have a wider range of experience of their children's involvement in decision-making than teachers have. They frequently act as important mediators for their children, not only with schools but also more generally within the local community. This can be a particularly significant part of their role when their children have special educational needs (Dale, 1996; Read, 2000). However, the shift from *advocacy* on behalf of their children to a supporting role with respect to their child's own *self-advocacy* is not necessarily an easy one for parents to put into effect, and it is evident that some parents would welcome explicit discussion with teachers and other parents about the issues involved.

Parents and teachers each have their own knowledge, understandings and experiences of children's decision-making. Children are likely to require the support of both if they are to participate as fully as possible in educational processes. For these reasons, it is argued in this book that there is a need to explore the relationship between the principles of parent partnership and pupil participation and further, that through acknowledging the potential tensions between these two principles, it is more likely that both parental and child perspectives will be given due weight.

Inclusive education and special educational needs

The book's central concerns with the development of parent partnership and pupil participation are located within the context of inclusive educational practice. The aim is to highlight both common issues and specific issues relating to children with special educational needs. Although the term 'special educational needs' is increasingly regarded as problematic by many writers, it remains current in both national and local policy frameworks, and for this reason is used throughout the book. According to the legal definition, children with special educational needs are regarded as those who 'have a learning difficulty which calls for special educational provision to be made for them' (Education Act, 1996, Section 312). Learning difficulty is further qualified by reference to significant difference from other children of the same age, or the presence of a disability which impedes access to educational facilities.

The conceptualisation of needs which underpins this rather circular definition is multifaceted. Debate continues about the processes involved and the relative importance of individual and environmental factors. However, there is a general consensus that the nature of the special educational needs that children experience arises in interaction between individual pupils and the demands which are made of them at school. It follows therefore that these needs are influenced by teacher–pupil relationships and by curricular and organisational factors within school. Schools do not, of course, operate in a social vacuum, and an understanding of special educational needs must also be informed by recognition of wider-ranging influences beyond the school environment, including societal and political values and expectations. From this brief summary it can be seen that current interpretations of the notion of special educational needs carry some subtlety and complexity, which have accumulated over the years since the term was introduced. Nevertheless, it is important to be alert to the nature of the reservations which are now being increasingly expressed about its usage.

It is only too apparent that any label which is applied to a minority group can become stigmatising and devaluing, and carries the risk of placing undue and negative emphasis on difference from the majority. Specific criticisms of the 'special educational needs' label highlight the way that it directs attention onto the individual as 'having' particular needs, thereby locating the problem within the child, rather than focusing on the barriers to children's learning that are implicated in the educational difficulties they experience (e.g. Hart, 1996; Booth, 1998).

While recognising the importance of the organisational, curricular and wider systemic barriers to learning that exist, however, there is no doubt that there are individual children who experience such difficulties in their learning at school that they require additional help if they are to make the most of their educational opportunities. Although some critics of the term 'special educational needs' would wish to abandon any label, others acknowledge that the use of a label can serve to identify those differences in children's needs which are sufficiently significant to require the safeguarding of additional resource allocation in order to meet them. Nevertheless, critics question what benefit there is in separating special educational needs from other forms of exceptional need. They point out that a range of common principles can be described that underpin aspects of provision for children with special educational needs and for those learning English as a second language, those who are exceptionally able, those whose needs arise from disrupted schooling, and so on (e.g. Davie, 1996).

Growing concern about a lack of clarity in current interpretations of the term 'special educational needs' is also reflected in Norwich's (1996) proposal of a unifying framework for considering the overlaps and boundaries between the full range of educational needs that children experience. Within this he distinguishes between common learning needs, which are shared with all of a child's peers; individual needs, which reflect the range of individual diversity found among all children; and exceptional needs, which arise from special characteristics or circumstances and which may be shared with a subgroup of peers. The exceptional needs he identifies include aspects of children's learning and emotional and behavioural difficulties, but also go well beyond current governmental policy definitions of special educational need.

The term 'exceptional needs' has been adopted by a number of writers, such as Mittler (2000), who finds the continuing use of the special educational needs label 'not only anachronistic but discriminatory' (p. 8). In his view, it serves to create a perception of a need for separate provision that is quite at odds with current policy initiatives to promote greater inclusiveness within education. This argument provides a useful reminder that concepts such as special educational needs and exceptionality are socially constructed, and cannot be viewed in isolation from the political and policy contexts in which they arise. It is therefore to be expected that not only our understandings of, but also our ways of referring to, significant aspects of individual difference will shift over time. However, although the government has acknowledged some of the problematic issues associated with present definitions and interpretations of special educational need (DfEE, 1998), it has nevertheless chosen to retain these in current legislation and guidance. Accordingly its policy has been one of clarification rather than re-formulation of terms, for example by distinguishing the boundaries and overlaps between the terms 'disability' and 'special educational need' (DfES, 2001a), and by proposing a framework for classifying different types of special educational need (DfES, 2003a).

The way in which we refer to children's needs carries subtle messages about what sort of provision we see as most appropriate for meeting those needs, and Mittler is not alone in linking his concerns about terminology to the question of inclusive education. Like others, he describes inclusive educational practice as necessitating 'a process of reform and restructuring of the school as a whole, with the aim of ensuring that all pupils can have access to the whole range of educational and social opportunities offered' (Mittler, 2000: 2). In other words, the essence of inclusive education can be characterised as a flexible and responsive school system which, as Wedell (1995) has argued, takes as its starting point a recognition of the diversity of pupils' needs. This perspective highlights two significant and complementary implications for the development of practice: first, that any attempt to implement inclusive education must embrace the needs of *all* pupils; but second, that for *some* of them, there is a risk of exclusion or marginalisation to be redressed.

This book attempts to engage with both these implications. Adopting Norwich's (1996) framework, it aims to address questions concerning principles and practices in the development of home–school relationships and pupil participation that are *common* across all children; it reflects upon the significance of *individual diversity;* and it gives explicit consideration to those *exceptional* issues that are distinctive to children with special educational needs.

Interrelationships

The ways in which the themes of the book interrelate with each other is best illustrated by reference to the ecological model of development proposed by Bronfenbrenner (1977). This model provides a convincing theoretical rationale for why home, school and the relationship between them are so significant for children's development. It also emphasises how important it is that the child be recognised as an active participant in both home and school contexts.

Bronfenbrenner describes an ecological framework for development that can be characterised as a nested system of environments. These environments are differentiated into four levels as outlined in Figure 1.1. At the innermost level is what he refers to as the microsystem, which is made up of the complex system of relationships that a developing child has with the immediate environments

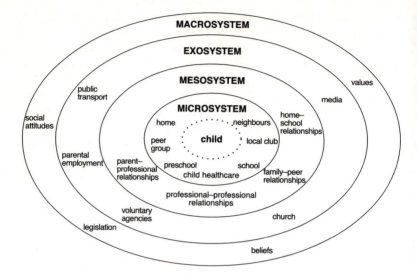

Figure 1.1 Bronfenbrenner's ecological framework (based on Bronfenbrenner, 1977, 1979)

in which he or she is living and learning. Bronfenbrenner is explicit that home is the primary learning context for most children within the microsystem, but further significant settings are likely to include preschool and school contexts, neighbourhood friends and peer groups and other local community contexts. For children with special educational needs, they may also include child health centres, speech and language therapy clinics and so on. Within each setting, Bronfenbrenner stresses that developing children are not passive recipients of their environmental experiences, but that they both influence and are influenced by their interactions in a process of 'progressive, mutual accommodation' (1977: 514). Accordingly, different children will experience the same environmental contexts differently because of their own active contribution to the interactions that take place.

The second level is referred to by Bronfenbrenner as the mesosystem. This system does not comprise discrete environmental settings, but is made up of the interrelationships between the most significant settings within an individual's microsystem. For children of school age, these include the relationships between home and school and peers, and in the case of those with special educational needs, may also include the relationships between the different professionals with whom they are involved. The significant aspect of this level of the model is that it emphasises that it is not only the interactions *within* immediate environmental settings, but also the interconnections *between* them, that are influential for children's development. Further, the stronger the links, the stronger the influence is likely to be. Where there are significant gaps in communication, for example, or in expectations and values, this will affect how well children are able to adapt to the learning demands that are made of them and how well supported they feel.

At the level of the mesosystem, therefore, Bronfenbrenner's model can be seen to provide a theoretical explanation of the significance of home–school relationships. In addition, where children are involved with a range of different professionals, it also demonstrates the importance of close inter-professional liaison. More tentatively, it is possible that where there are clear interconnections within the mesosystem, this can contribute to children's sense of belonging and of identity, so that they perceive themselves as a part of, and included within, local networks at school and beyond. For these reasons it can be argued that all these interrelationships are particularly important for those whose development and learning are at risk, and those who are vulnerable to marginalisation in school or local community.

At the third and fourth levels of his model, Bronfenbrenner seeks to explain the effect of broader environmental influences on children's development. The third level, or exosystem, consists of social structures that 'impinge on' what goes on in the micro- and mesosystems. It includes, for example, statutory and voluntary agencies, public transport, parental employment, church, media and so on. It has been noted previously in this chapter that public transport and parental employment arrangements can serve to restrict the extent of parental contact with school. Taking another example from this level, local LEA policy can influence a school's approach to parental involvement and community links, or determine its experiences of inclusive educational practice, in ways which impact on a child both directly and indirectly. As Dockrell (1997) has observed with respect to children with special educational needs, aspects of the exosystem 'can potentially offer a range of supports which allows children and young people with special needs to participate fully in activities, or they can serve to marginalise and distance them' (p. 114).

The outermost level, referred to as the macrosystem, represents the prevailing ideology of the time. It includes legislative and policy frameworks, social attitudes, values and beliefs, which affect actions and interactions at other levels of the model. With respect to children, their parents and others involved in their care, Bronfenbrenner explains the significance of the macrosystem as follows:

> what place or priority children and those responsible for their care have in such macrosystems is of special importance in determining how a child and his or her caretakers are treated and interact with each other in different types of settings.
>
> (Bronfenbrenner, 1977: 515)

The same reasoning can be applied where children have particular needs: the model provides a framework against which to consider, for example, the ways in which societal attitudes and beliefs concerning special educational needs and disability have an impact on political discourse about rights, advocacy, self-advocacy and inclusion; and how these then translate into national legislation, local policy and practice.

Policy frameworks that are of particular relevance to the themes of this book are reviewed in Chapter 2. Although specific English policy developments are highlighted, attention is also drawn to the principles underpinning these which, together with questions concerning implementation, have an applicability to a wider range of contexts. Attitudes, values and beliefs are central to much that follows, and permeate the discussion throughout. Following on from the overview of policy, the rest of the book focuses particularly on the microsystem of home and the mesosystem of the home–school relationship. Parenting and family are central to the development of much social and educational policy, reflecting a political belief in the primary significance of children's home lives for their subsequent development. Chapter 3 explores the nature of the learning contexts that home and family represent, through a consideration of roles and relationships as well as incidental and more explicit learning opportunities. It highlights aspects of family diversity, including those associated with special educational needs and disability. Chapter 4 looks at the relationship between the informal learning contexts of home and formal schooling in order to consider the extent to which gaps and disjunctures here may be implicated in the patterns of educational disadvantage experienced by some children. It goes on to consider contrasting initiatives that aim to combat educational disadvantage, and the implications that can be drawn from these for the development of home–school links. The active promotion of positive home–school relationships is the focus of Chapter 5. This addresses the development of effective communication between home and school as well as more active forms of collaboration, drawing attention both to general issues and to those that are specific to parents and children with special educational needs. Consideration of the ways in which the home–school relationship changes and develops over time, and the place of the child in the relationship, form a link to Chapter 6, which is concerned with the promotion of children's active participation in decision-making both at home and at school. The concluding chapter offers a reflection upon the principles of partnership and participation, and on their practical implementation within the context of inclusive educational practice.

Note

1 Throughout the book, the term 'parent' will be used to refer to parents, foster parents and others who fulfil the primary caregiving role for children. It can be argued that the home–school relationship is of particular importance for children in foster care and other forms of public care (e.g. Coulling, 2000; DfEE, 2000).

Chapter 2

Developing policy frameworks

This chapter is primarily concerned with the educational policy frameworks for the development of home–school partnership, children's participation and inclusion. However, as the previous discussion of Bronfenbrenner's (1977) model makes clear, schools do not operate in isolation from broader societal contexts, and accordingly it is important first to briefly trace some interconnections with relevant dimensions of social policy concerning children and families.

Since 1997, when the New Labour government came into power, one central focus of policy development has been the reduction of social exclusion coupled with the promotion of social inclusion. Social exclusion refers to inequalities in society, in particular those associated with poverty, but also embraces broader social and cultural issues. Accordingly, the strategies for promoting social inclusion are concerned with strengthening communities as well as with material resources (Riddell and Tett, 2001). Because of the multiplicity of interacting factors that can serve as obstacles to social inclusion, an emphasis has been placed on the sort of 'joined-up' thinking which facilitates coordinated inter-agency working. Education has a key role to play in this agenda: among the particular strategies identified by the government are raising attainments, lowering rates of non-attendance and school exclusion, and the development of inclusive educational practice. However, as Mittler (2000: 45) has observed:

> The process of working towards a more inclusive society has to start long before children first go to school. Its foundations lie in a society in which parents can feel supported, both economically and socially, in bringing up a family, a society in

which children are valued and cherished and in which they can flourish.

It is not surprising, therefore, to find that two essential strands to government policy are associated with parenting and the family, and with children's rights and services.

The framework for family policy was presented in the Green Paper, *Supporting Families* (Home Office, 1998). It includes the provision of information and advice, for example through the National Family and Parenting Institute and parent helplines. There are also a range of financial initiatives, such as the Children's Tax Credit and the Working Families' Tax Credit which, together with the introduction of 'family friendly' employment practices, are aimed at reducing child poverty. Support for the parental role in bringing up their children primarily takes the form of a range of inter-agency, community-based early intervention programmes. Most of these, including parenting programmes and the Sure Start initiative, are targeted at families living in disadvantaged areas; they are also available for families of disabled children and those with special educational needs. These initiatives (which are discussed in detail in Chapter 4) seem to be underpinned by an acknowledgement of the complex interacting influences on children's development and family functioning that were discussed by Bronfenbrenner (1997). However, by contrast, when children demonstrate problems such as truancy or anti-social behaviour, policy appears to be premised on far more simplistic notions of parental influence and control. In these cases, the government takes a more controversial approach whereby, rather than support, parents can expect to become the focus for blame and to be penalised for their children's misdemeanours. A recent analysis of family policy (Henricson, 2003) draws attention to the resulting tensions and, while rightly acknowledging the extent of governmental commitment to the provision of support, highlights the need to present clearer and more consistent messages concerning parental rights and responsibilities.

In parallel with this emphasis on parenting and family support, there has also been a growing recognition of the rights of children. The 1989 UN Convention on the Rights of the Child (UN, 1989, Article 12) states that children have the right to express their views on issues that affect them, and to have those views listened to and taken seriously. The 1989 Children Act, which focuses on support for children in need, incorporates this principle, together with an explicit acknowledgement that child and parent perspectives can differ. In doing so, it highlights the linkage between parental rights and those of their children: that is, an endorsement of children's rights inevitably has an impact on those of their parents. Within the context of educational provision, for example, Henricson (2003) has observed that the Personal, Social and Health Education (PSHE) curriculum in schools, and the access to personal development advice that is offered to all 13- to 19-year-old pupils by the Connexions service (which aims to prepare pupils for the transition to work and adult life), could both be seen as encroaching on parental autonomy. In a similar vein, Freeman (2000) notes that critics of the advocacy of children's rights argue that these can act to undermine the family as a whole, and in particular, that they have a negative impact on parents' ability to take decisions. Further, as Roche (1996) highlights, tensions can exist between policies that assert children's rights and different cultural family values. He points out:

> It is one thing for us to declare that children have certain rights, it is quite another to persuade the different communities in our society of the rightness of this declaration especially when it can be read as undermining key beliefs and values and when the very language of rights, let alone children's rights, is seen as inappropriate in the context of notions of family life in the respective communities.
>
> (Roche, 1996: 34)

Despite the potentially problematic relationship between a focus on children's rights and the values of the family contexts in which some children are brought up, however, the principle of children's participation is strongly emphasised in certain aspects of current policy. Thus, for example, participation has been identified as a critical part of its core strategy by the government's Children and Young People's Unit, who assert that:

> We want to hear the voices of young people, influencing and shaping local services; contributing to their local communities; feeling heard; feeling valued; being treated as responsible citizens.
>
> (CYPU, 2000: 26)

To further this intention, the government has commissioned research into the nature and extent of existing participatory practice (Kirby *et al.*, 2003). Such an explicit acknowledgement of rights to participate can be viewed as particularly significant for those who are at risk of exclusion (Roche, 1996), and is therefore consistent with the attempt to promote social inclusion. From this perspective, it is relevant to note that, although there is comparatively little in educational policy that is specifically related to children's rights, most of this is to be found in the particular context of special educational needs.

Set against this broad policy overview, the rest of this chapter traces the development of educational policy as it relates to home–school relationships and children's participation. In discussing these themes, specific developments concerning children with special educational needs are highlighted. The chapter concludes with an overview of inclusive education policy and considers the role of parent partnership and children's participation in developing inclusive practice.

The development of educational policy on home–school relationships

As noted in the previous chapter, there has been a long-standing recognition within educational policy of the importance of positive home–school relationships in the education of all children. A wide range of governmental reports, dating back to the Plowden Report (DES, 1967) and continuing to current times, emphasises the role that parental involvement has to play in children's education. The original rationale for seeking to build closer home–school relationships was based on an accumulation of evidence that there were enhanced academic outcomes for children when their parents and teachers worked together collaboratively. However, a different political imperative directed the development of policy in the 1980s and 1990s. Throughout this period, an emphasis was placed on making schools more accountable to parents and educational legislation was introduced which focused on extending parental rights in significant ways. These rights, which were summarised in a 'Parents' Charter' (DfE, 1994a), included the right to information about the school's curriculum, policies, procedures and performance outcomes as indicated by formal assessment results; the right to information about their own children's progress and achievements; the right to express a preference for a particular school placement; and the right to be involved to a certain extent in the management of the school through parental representation on the governing body. Arrangements for monitoring the ways in which schools interact with their pupils' parents were also built into the inspection framework, which incorporates a review of parental perceptions of school practice.

There is no doubt that this legislation played a valuable role in encouraging greater openness and clearer communication of information from schools to pupils' parents, and in promoting a view of home–school liaison as an integral part of the educational process, rather than an optional extra. Nevertheless, it also accentuated some fundamental tensions concerning parent–teacher relationships because it was premised on the notion that educational services should operate as a quasi-market system in which parents were to be viewed as consumers. It is inevitable in their dealings with school that parents will be first and foremost concerned to achieve what they believe to be best for their own child. However, there is a distinct difference for both parents and teachers between a relationship characterised by individual consumerism and one based on collaborative educational partnership. There is a real tension between the principles of equity and choice: that is, because some parents are more effective than others in the role of consumers, this almost inevitably leads to inequitable treatment. Despite the rhetoric of choice, in practice there is not a great deal of scope for parental preferences to be followed within the school system, and there is evidence that professional parents are more likely than others to be successful in exercising their rights in order to obtain the resources they want for their children (Martin, 2000). Moreover, as discussed later, a policy of competition in a quasi-market place can also cause particular difficulties for parents of children with special educational needs.

Following the change in government in 1997, further shifts in policy have taken place. The strengthening of parental rights has continued, for example through parental representation on local authority education committees. The government has also increased the range of information it provides for parents, both through printed booklets and on dedicated websites. At the same time, though, an attempt has been made to couple rights with responsibilities, as exemplified in the requirement, introduced from 1999, for schools to draw up written home–school agreements with parents. In principle, home–school agreements can offer a vehicle for three-way discussions between children, parents and teachers about expectations, communication, roles and responsibilities. However, there is little evidence to date of them being used so constructively and there are several problematic issues that need to be addressed if they are to operate in a way that supports the notion of a partnership between home and school. Vincent (2000), for example, argues that although framed in terms of two-way commitments, they are based on the assumption that the parental role is primarily to support an agenda set by the school. She observes that governmental guidance conveys a view of 'an approved fashion' (p. 24) in which parents should act, for example by monitoring their children's homework and attending parents' evenings, which is easier to fulfil for those who are living in comfortable material circumstances. She also points out that typically the commitments made by the school are, first, far less explicit than those that children and parents are asked to agree to; and second, mainly focused on undertakings that should be made anyway, regardless of the level of support from home.

It can be seen that the development of policy, with its evolving focus on rights and responsibilities, still leaves unresolved a number of questions and dilemmas concerning the reciprocal accountability of parents and teachers in relation to children's education. However, this should not distract attention from the reasons for seeking to promote positive home–school relationships. The educational basis for the principle of home–school partnership stems not just from an acknowledgement of parental rights, but from the recognition that home is a primary context for children's learning, and that schools must seek to build on and extend the learning experiences of home if they are to be fully effective. In order to do so, this requires the development of a relationship that encourages genuine two-way communication.

Home–school relationships and children with special educational needs

Home–school relationships are important for all children, but Bronfenbrenner's (1977) ecological model highlights their increased significance for those whose development and learning are at risk.

The impact of learning difficulties on children's attainments, social interactions and behaviour is influenced by the nature and extent of the support they experience, and it is evident that they are likely to make best progress when their parents and teachers share a positive commitment to meeting their needs. This argument was put forward very strongly in the Warnock Report (DES, 1978), where partnership with parents is described as essential. A full chapter of the report is dedicated to the question of parent–professional relationships, and opens with these words:

> The successful education of children with special educational needs is dependent upon the full involvement of their parents: indeed, unless the parents are seen as equal partners in the educational process, then the purpose of our report will be frustrated.
>
> (DES, 1978, para 9.1)

This unequivocal endorsement of the role of parents as 'equal partners' in the education of their children presented challenges to schools, for it has not been unusual for teachers to more readily view parents as 'part of the problem' in relation to children's educational needs rather than as partners with a unique contribution to make. Croll and Moses (1985) in their study of primary schools, for example, found that teachers frequently ascribed children's learning difficulties, and almost always ascribed their behavioural difficulties, to home circumstances. It is evident that teachers' knowledge and understanding of the complex nature of special educational needs have progressed since then, and in their more recent research, Croll and Moses (2000) report that teachers have generally become more circumspect in identifying the causes of children's difficulties. Nevertheless, in the case of a quarter of children with learning difficulties and more than half of those with emotional and behavioural difficulties, teachers ascribed their special educational needs to factors at home. Parents are typically well-aware that teachers make judgements about their parenting on the basis of their children's attainments and behaviour in school, and there is little doubt that when negative assumptions exist, these must interfere with the development of constructive home–school relationships.

The difficulty in exercising parental choice with respect to school placement can be exacerbated when a child has learning difficulties (Evans and Vincent, 1997), and as a result, for some parents the relationship with school may already be fraught before their child is admitted. Even in a policy climate that is in principle supportive of inclusion, parents often have to argue the case for their children to access mainstream education. As Bailey (1998: 177) has observed:

> Many parents have had to fight long and frustrating battles to have their children accepted into regular education. These parents have often been regarded as trouble-makers because of their determination to get what is best for their children. In many cases, they have suffered extreme stress and anxiety.

In such situations, if positive home–school relationships are to be developed, then there is an evident need for both sensitivity and commitment on the part of schools in order to reassure and build parents' confidence about the support that they and their children can expect to receive.

Despite the obstacles to home–school relationships that exist in practice, the principles that were embodied in the Warnock Report have, over time, become firmly established in policy. Immediately following the publication of the report, legislation focused primarily on the minority of children with a statement of special educational needs. This introduced parental rights to participate in the associated statutory assessment procedures and in the annual reviews that take place when their child has a statement. It quickly became apparent that parents required better information and support if they were to make a significant contribution to these processes (Sandow et al., 1987; Vaughan, 1989). It was also clear that the emphasis on children with statements and their parents had left a lack of clarity and consistency concerning policy across the rest of the continuum of special educational needs. However, it was not until the 1993 Education Act (subsequently incorporated into the 1996 Education Act) that these two issues began to be addressed. With regard to the first, parents' rights in assessment procedures were strengthened, access was provided to a Named Person who could provide information and help to take up their rights, and a right of appeal to an independent Special Educational Needs Tribunal was introduced. The second issue was addressed by the introduction of the Code of Practice (DfE, 1994b), which aimed to provide a unifying framework of guidance on provision for the full range of special educational needs.

Inequities remain in the system: among parents of children with special educational needs, just as among any other group of parents, some are demonstrably more effective than others in taking up their rights. For example, Gross (1996) has presented evidence to show that it is the most articulate and best supported parents who gain additional resources for their children through their involvement in statementing procedures. Further legislation has therefore aimed to reinforce and extend the nature of the services available to all parents. All local education authorities have been required to establish Parent Partnership Services which offer parents information, advice and support (Wolfendale and Cook, 1997), as well as arrangements for resolving disagreements. Where disagreements between parents and education authorities persist, the brief of the independent tribunal has been widened to address disability discrimination and has been renamed the SEN and Disability Tribunal.

For both schools and local education authorities, the original Code of Practice (DfE 1994b) and its subsequent revision (DfES, 2001a) elaborate on the ways in which they should seek to develop their relationships with the parents of all children with special educational needs. Partnership with parents is described as a fundamental principle of the Code, and parents' groups are reported to have responded positively to its emphasis on consultation and collaboration (Friel, 1997; Russell, 1997). The Code highlights the importance of early identification of special educational need, and outlines a continuous and progressive cycle of assessment, planning, action and review, which should be characterised at all stages by partnerships not only between school staff, parents and local education authorities, but also with other professionals where appropriate. It is intended as practical guidance for schools and local education authorities, who are legally bound to 'have regard' to its provisions. Not surprisingly, the priority in implementing the Code for many schools became the development of the within-school systems for assessment, individual educational plans (IEPs), monitoring and review that were required. As a result, at least in the early stages, not all schools addressed the expectations of the Code concerning the full involvement of parents in these processes (Beveridge, 1997).

This gap between policy and practice has been implicitly acknowledged in the revised Code of Practice, which includes more detailed guidance for schools concerning communication with parents. The principle of working in partnership with parents is reiterated as follows:

All parents of children with special educational needs should be treated as partners. They should be supported so as to be able and empowered to:

- recognise and fulfil their responsibilities as parents and play an active and valued role in their children's education
- have knowledge of their child's entitlement within the SEN framework
- make their views known about how their child is educated
- have access to information, advice and support during assessment and any related decision-making processes about special educational provision.

(DfES, 2001a: 16)

This extract serves to highlight the emphasis within current policy that parents not only require information, but may also require support, if they are to take up their rights in relation to their children's education. It also illustrates the same unresolved tensions between rights and responsibilities that have previously been discussed within mainstream policy developments: the rhetoric is of empowerment, but the linkage with responsibilities is not made clear.

The development of educational policy on children's participation

There is increasing recognition in many schools of the importance of promoting children's active participation in decision-making. At an individual level, this is evidenced by pupil involvement in target-setting and monitoring of their own progress, and at whole-school level, developments include School Councils, peer mediation strategies, involvement in anti-bullying procedures, and so on. However, despite the emphasis placed on children's participation by the Children and Young People's Unit as referred to earlier, it is surprisingly absent from much educational policy.

The Elton Report on discipline in schools (DES, 1989) was published in the same year as the Children Act and was perhaps similarly influenced by the UN Convention on the Rights of Children, for it made a strong recommendation that pupils should be involved in the process of development and review of school behaviour policies. More recently, two further developments within the context of mainstream policy also have the potential for promoting pupil participation. First, as already indicated, home–school agreements can act as a basis for involving both children and their parents in three-way discussions with teachers about expectations and mutual commitments. It must be acknowledged, though, that there is as yet little evidence of much active pupil participation in practice (Edwards, 2002). Second, the introduction of a citizenship curriculum offers some possibilities. Researchers such as Alderson (2002) have expressed their disappointment that national documentation on citizenship education does not explicitly address children's rights but, nevertheless, the curriculum should provide pupils with the sort of knowledge that strengthens their capacity to make informed choices and participate in decision-making (Wyness, 2000).

Particular issues arise for children with special educational needs and disabilities if they are to participate in educational processes. The UN Convention refers to the need to give due weight to children's views according to age, maturity and capability. Rose (1998) is among those who have pointed out that this clause could too easily be used to exclude children with some forms of special educational need from participation. He argues that there is a real risk that, where there are severe communication difficulties for example, children may be judged not capable of expressing their views. As Thomas and his colleagues have pointed out:

> To be both a child and disabled . . . conjoins characteristics which are doubly disadvantaging as far as having one's voice heard is concerned.
>
> (Thomas *et al.*, 1998: 18)

It is perhaps for this reason that more explicit attempts have been made to develop policy for the participation of children in special educational provision than has so far been the case elsewhere.

The original Code of Practice (DfE, 1994b) proposed that children should be involved to the greatest extent possible in assessment, planning and review processes. However, it neither highlighted nor elaborated on the principle of pupil participation, and on the whole, there was little impact on school practice (Rose *et al.*, 1996). It became apparent, therefore, that there was a need for more explicit emphasis and guidance. This has been acknowledged within the revised Code (DfES, 2001a), where pupil participation is given the full weight of a specific chapter. Section 4 of the associated SEN Toolkit (DfES, 2001b) expands in more detail on principles and whole-school strategies designed to promote successful pupil participation, and provides some specific ideas and examples to support the development of teachers' practice. In recognition of schools' needs for further support materials, the government has also expressed its commitment to the publication of more practical tools in the future (DfES, 2004).

The Code points out that children with special educational needs not only have the right to be involved in educational decisions that affect them, but also have unique perspectives and insights to contribute. They should therefore be viewed as important participants in assessment processes, discussions about choice of school, the setting of learning targets, the development of IEPs and annual reviews. For schools to implement this, an emphasis is placed on the need to ensure that children 'feel confident that they will be listened to and that their views are valued' (DfES, 2001a: 27). At the same time, the Code quotes from the Children Act 1989, with the precautionary note that there is 'a fine balance between giving the child a voice and encouraging them to make informed decisions, and overburdening them with decision-making procedures where they have insufficient experience and knowledge to make appropriate judgements without additional support' (DfES, 2001a: 27).

In requiring that the individual perspectives of both parents and their children are sought and respected in all aspects of decision-making, the Code makes considerable demands on professional skills and sensitivity. The SEN Toolkit (DfES, 2001b) is explicit that professionals will sometimes need to advocate for children to ensure that their voices are heard, but it is important to remember that parents themselves are also used to acting in this role. There are always potential difficulties in trying to ensure that parents feel that their views are given equal weight to those of professionals. The question of the status afforded to different views becomes even more complex when children are also included in discussion. These issues are heightened during the process of planning the transition to post-school experiences, where it appears that practice so far falls short of the Code's high expectations. Transition planning procedures for young people with statements begin with initial discussions during the Year 9 annual review and continue on a yearly basis until the student leaves school. The transition period can be one of uncertainty and anxiety for both students and their parents, but Dee's research (2000, 2002) describes planning meetings in which the degree of procedural formality often precludes any real engagement with their concerns and hopes for the future. Further, the imbalance in status afforded to the views and preferences of the different participants leads Dee to conclude that transition planning is at present one of the least successful aspects of the Code's implementation.

The Code of Practice does include some acknowledgement of the difficulties in establishing a satisfactory balance in educational decision-making processes between attention to children's rights, parents' rights and professional responsibilities. It argues that these difficulties are most likely to be resolved when there are constructive home–school relationships in place.

The promotion of inclusive education

Concepts of inclusion and inclusive education have developed over time within the context of broader social values and political priorities. When the Warnock Report (DES, 1978) was published, it used the term 'integration' to refer to the involvement in mainstream school of those children with special educational needs who had traditionally been educated in segregated provision. It distinguished between different forms of integration: locational, when children with special educational needs share a site with mainstream pupils; social, when they also share social out-of-class activities; and functional, when they join in at least some mainstream lessons. This very simple model quickly became associated with narrow interpretations of what integration involved. It appeared to endorse a step-by-step progression, where children who could demonstrate their suitability might gradually move towards full involvement in mainstream provision. The emphasis was placed on *where* education took place, rather than on its quality. Further, there was little recognition that, if integration was to be successful, this had implications for mainstream approaches for *all* pupils: instead the onus was placed on individual children with special educational needs to 'fit in' to existing school structures that had not been designed with their needs in mind.

Dissatisfaction with such limited views of the nature of integration grew as a result of a number of factors. First, there was increasing acknowledgement of the interactive nature of special educational needs, and therefore of the important contribution that curricular and organisational factors can make to the learning difficulties that children experience. In parallel with this, a social model of disability began to have increasing influence (e.g. Barton *et al.*, 2002). Instead of focusing on individuals and individual problems, this model stresses that disability has to be understood as a function of disabling social processes. At school level, these ways of understanding special educational needs and disability have clear implications, for both highlight the need to develop practices and procedures that are responsive to and value diversity, rather than viewing difference as problematic. A further related impetus for change came from the argument, put particularly strongly by disabled activists and associated organisations, that participation in mainstream community services raises fundamental questions of human rights. From this perspective, the main obstacles to participation derive from a lack of respect for such rights (e.g. Roaf, 2002), and therefore the onus is not on the individual to demonstrate a capacity to access mainstream services, but on the development of services which are accessible by all.

These shifts towards a broader understanding were reflected in growing use of the term 'inclusion'. Whereas integration had too often been understood as referring simply to the movement of children with special educational needs into mainstream school, the term 'inclusion' focused on wider questions of educational reform. Attention was directed to the ways in which existing educational structures and processes could serve to disadvantage and marginalise particular groups and what could be done to change this. As a result, the promotion of inclusive educational practice became seen as centrally concerned with increasing schools' responsiveness to diversity in ways which both enhance the participation of all of their pupils and, at the same time, offer support as necessary for those groups most vulnerable to exclusion.

In line with these evolving concepts of integration and inclusion, the associated policy frameworks also started with a focus on children with special educational needs and where they were to be educated. An explicit acknowledgement of human rights arguments and more complex notions of inclusive education have been much more recent developments. Thus, the 1981 Education Act stated that children with special educational needs should be educated in mainstream schools, provided that certain conditions were met. First, the views of the child's parents must be taken into account. Not all wish for inclusion, for some parents feel strongly that their children require specialist schooling in order to meet their needs.

It is evident, therefore, that respect for parental views will have an impact on the nature and level of inclusive educational provision (see, for example, Norwich, 2000). At the same time, it is important to acknowledge that in practice parental choice has not always been a reality. Simmons (2000), for example, has reported on how far placement in mainstream school has depended on the age and assessed needs of the child, where the family lives and, very often, 'parental energy and commitment' (p. 257). This is because local education authorities have been able to circumvent parental wishes on the basis of the other conditions, which until their recent amendment, have remained in the legislation for twenty years. These conditions are that placement in a mainstream school must be compatible with the child receiving the special provision required; with the effective education of the other pupils in the school; and with the efficient use of resources.

A significant shift in policy came about in 1997 with the change of government, which presented for consultation a wide-ranging programme for special educational needs (DfEE, 1997a), in which it explicitly endorsed the principle of inclusion not only on educational, but also on moral, rights-based and social grounds. In line with its commitment to a social inclusion agenda, the then Secretary of State for Education argued: 'We must develop inclusive schools if we want to lay the foundations for an inclusive society' (Blunkett, 1997: 150). In 2001, the government introduced the Special Educational Needs and Disability Act as well as the revised Code of Practice (DfES, 2001a). The legislation couples frameworks on provision for special educational needs with disability discrimination measures which, among other things, make it unlawful to discriminate against disabled pupils in admissions to and education at school. Parental wishes for their children with special educational needs to attend mainstream school are to be agreed in all but the minority of cases where it would be incompatible with the efficient education of other pupils. With respect to the quality of educational experiences, the Code provides links to the National Curriculum statement on inclusion, which sets out principles teachers should follow in making curricular provision more inclusive. Schools have also been supplied with the Index for Inclusion (Centre for Studies in Inclusive Education, 2000), a set of materials designed to involve schools in self-review and development planning in order to promote greater inclusiveness. This is in line with proposed government strategy to require schools to make inclusive practice an integral part of their self-evaluation (DfES, 2004). It is notable that the Index, as well as the government's inspection framework for evaluating inclusion (OFSTED, 2001), both take a broad stance that not only incorporates a focus on special educational needs and disability, but also deals with a wide range of other disadvantaged groups.

Roche (1996: 37) has argued that 'it is only through respect for children and their perspectives that a real community of interests, which includes all those who live within it, can come about'. A respect for pupils based on a genuine valuing of their diversity is frequently characterised as an essential part of an inclusive school ethos or culture (Dyson *et al.*, 2003). What is also required is a commitment to the learning of all pupils, for as Florian (1998) has emphasised, inclusion is not a question of simply making mainstream opportunities available: rather it necessitates school practices that facilitate active participation. Pupil participation is thus central to current understandings of inclusive education. The Index for Inclusion, for example, states:

> Inclusion in education involves the processes of increasing the participation of students in, and reducing their exclusion from, the cultures, curricula and communities of local schools.
> (Centre for Studies in Inclusive Education, 2000: 12)

The learning community of school goes beyond pupils and staff, however, and must also be seen to embrace the pupils' parents. Parents of children with special educational needs have unique perspectives on inclusion both within and beyond school, and their role in pushing forward inclusive policy and practice has often been a significant one (Evans, 2000). Further, Gartner and Lipsky (1999) have reported that it is a characteristic of successful inclusion initiatives that they develop creative ways of involving parents as 'an integral part' of the school community. There is an increasing consensus, therefore, that parental involvement is an essential factor in the development of inclusive educational practice.

Summary

This overview of current policy frameworks demonstrates the extent to which active participation by children and their parents is central to social and educational inclusion agendas. A number of unresolved issues relating to parental rights and responsibilities that run through family policies have been highlighted. Further questions concern the interface between children's rights, parental autonomy and family functioning.

For schools, there is a clear requirement to establish constructive working partnerships with their pupils' parents. Formulations of the home–school relationship are, however, complicated because the lasting policy legacy of 'parents as consumers' is in fundamental tension with concepts of 'parents as partners' in a collaborative educational endeavour. The challenges faced by schools in seeking to work in partnership with parents are potentially further complicated by the promotion of their children's active participation in decision-making processes. This may be one reason why it is that, as parental rights have been increasingly strengthened in relation to their children's education, comparatively little attention has been paid to children's rights until recently. Attempts to demonstrate how policy initiatives on both parent partnership and pupil participation might be translated into practice have been more extensive in the context of special educational needs than in general education policy. While not problem-free, the guidance provided by the Code of Practice does provide a starting point for developing procedures that have a far wider whole-school applicability.

Looking beyond governmental guidance, the implementation of policy must be informed by an understanding of the educational grounds for seeking to develop home–school partnerships. The positive collaborative relationship between parents and teachers that is considered so important for children's progress must be underpinned by an appreciation of the significance of the parental role in children's development. The nature of the learning context that home and family represent is the subject of the next chapter.

Chapter 3

Home and family
Contexts for learning

Home and family play a key role in children's development and learning. The intimate and profound emotional relationships that are characteristic of families set the context within which children develop their identities as daughters or sons, sisters or brothers, nieces or nephews and grandchildren. Families typically act to provide care and support, and to socialise children into the values and culture of their community. Children are not only recipients of socialisation processes, though, but are active participants who influence as well as are influenced by the dynamics of life at home.

The patterns of family life that children experience reflect wider social trends. Clarke (1996), for example, describes ways in which changing ideas about marriage and divorce, gender roles, maternal employment, child rearing and child care, have led to significant changes in family structures. It is not rare for children to experience a degree of family change and instability at some point in their childhood and, while most children in the UK live with their parents, Clarke highlights the growing minority who live with a lone parent or in a reconstituted family. It is clearly the case that differing family structures will offer children a different range of social experiences and relationships, both within and beyond the family. From their review of research in this area, McGurk and Soriano (1998) conclude that what is most significant for children's development is the quality of the care they receive rather than the particular family structure. They argue that children thrive best in situations where there is at least one adult who is unconditionally committed to their well-being, and where that adult feels supported in the parenting role.

Researchers who have sought to elicit children's perspectives on their home life (e.g. Goodnow and Burns, 1985; Morrow, 1998;

Brannen *et al.*, 2000) have reported that they themselves highlight the significance of the unconditional nature of family relationships, and view these as providing security and emotional support. In Goodnow and Burns's study, this is explicitly contrasted with the evaluative relationships children experience in school. Children's concepts of family can go beyond relatives to include a wide range of people and pets who are important to them. Essential elements for their perceptions of family membership appear to be a feeling of belonging and relationships that are based on mutual care and support.

The context of home comprises a wide range of activities and opportunities for learning. The main focus of this chapter is on significant family relationships and their contribution to children's development. After considering common patterns in parent–child interactions and wider family relations, particular issues are high-lighted that relate to special educational needs. The chapter con-cludes with a consideration of the range of diversity in children's experiences at home, and the implications of this diversity for schools.

Parents as facilitators of their children's development

Children's learning at home is rooted in social relationships, of which the most influential is that with their parents. An extensive body of literature has described the ways in which parents provide the sorts of stimulation that lay the foundations for subsequent social, emotional, physical and intellectual growth. Bronfenbrenner (1979: 60) has summarised the process of facilitating learning in the following terms:

> Learning and development are facilitated by the participation of the developing person in progressively more complex patterns of reciprocal activity with someone with whom that person has developed a strong and enduring emotional attachment and when the balance of power gradually shifts in favor of the developing person.

The elements that he identifies here:

1   active participation in progressively more complex activities;

2   during reciprocal, mutually influencing interactions which are underpinned by a strong affective bond; and
3   where the learner is supported to become increasingly self-directing over time.

have all been associated with the developing parent–child relationship.

From their earliest interactions onwards, parents act as though their babies' behaviours have meaning, and in doing so, create a context for two-way communication. These interactions are typically characterised by a strong emotional intimacy and mutual involvement, and observational research has shown them to be closely synchronised. Initially the fine-tuning and sequencing of their vocal and non-verbal 'dialogue' is largely supported by parental actions, but very quickly children also begin to initiate and sustain interactions. Thus parents and children reciprocally follow one another's lead, and this mutual responsiveness is seen to be particularly important, not only in developing the principles of interactive turn-taking, but also in establishing the affective base from which children derive confidence to explore their environment.

Beyond the context of these early intimate interactions, parental responsiveness to their child's actions in play and teaching contexts has also been the subject of much research. Parents have been described as using 'scaffolding' techniques to support and extend their children's activities. For example, in early play sequences such as ball-rolling or brick-building, they often use strategies to orient their children towards the game, followed by prompts and cues as needed to engage their play. Then, as their children become more practised and begin to take more control over the way the play develops, parents fade their prompts, but may introduce new demands to make the game more challenging. Parents vary, of course, in the quality of their scaffolding techniques and studies have focused on the relationship between the support they give and their children's subsequent achievements. From her review of the literature, Meadows (1996) concludes that, where parental scaffolding is flexibly responsive to their children's behaviour, this gives rise to the most effective learning. However, she also points out that, in order to interpret this finding, there are reciprocal influences between parents and children that need to be taken into account: that is, 'Parents may well differ in their responsiveness to children, but children also differ in their ability to provoke useful responses' (p. 45).

The scaffolding strategies just described are very similar to those used by professional teachers with young children, and indeed, in some of the research studies reviewed by Meadows, parents have been asked to explicitly teach their children a particular task. However, this does not imply that parents necessarily make conscious use of teaching techniques. More typically, their conversational and interactive play sequences tend to be natural and spontaneous, arising from shared activities and daily routines, and are often initiated by their children. The picture that emerges from research therefore is one of parents acting as facilitators more than as explicit instructors of their children.

As their children move through the preschool and early school years, however, a number of studies (e.g. Tizard *et al.*, 1988) report that many parents also begin to adopt more specific teaching intentions, for example in relation to early literacy, numeracy and self-care skills. This does not necessarily mean that they all share similar perceptions about what it is that constitutes teaching, or about its place as part of the parental role. For example, Atkin and Bastiani (1986) identify three dimensions of difference in the views expressed by parents of primary school children. In their study, parents vary in the extent to which they believe that teaching:

1   is primarily concerned with systematically planned and adult-directed activity or also incorporates more incidental and child-initiated interaction;
2   involves the use of tasks and methods with a specifically educational focus or also embraces improvised approaches and materials;
3   requires a formal learning context or can take place anywhere within the context of daily routines.

Their beliefs will clearly influence the approach that parents take in facilitating their children's learning: nevertheless it is evident that a great deal of incidental teaching continues to go on at home during the primary school years, even when parents do not see their role as one that incorporates explicit tuition.

There is less information concerning patterns of parental support for learning during the secondary school years. Montandon's (2001) research with 11–12-year-olds in Geneva suggests that many expect their parents to provide them with guidance and teaching, and it seems reasonable to suppose that parents may remain a significant influence throughout their children's schooling. Any direct assistance with the homework set by school is clearly likely to vary with their child's growing independence, and with their own feelings of competence to help. However, Crozier (2000) has reported that among British 11–16-year-olds, almost all say that their parents help at least some of the time with their homework, and Bates and Wilson (2003) have described continuing parental involvement among the 16–19-year-old age group that they studied.

It is beyond the scope of this book to consider in detail the issues involved in home-based schooling (see, for example, Meighan, 1992, 1997). However, it is currently estimated that approximately 1 per cent of children in the UK are educated at home rather than in school (Home Education UK, 2003). In concluding this consideration of the parental role in relation to learning, therefore, it is appropriate to reflect that in addition to the large numbers of parents who are active in supporting schoolwork throughout the primary and secondary school years, there is also a small percentage who choose to exercise their responsibilities for their children's education directly themselves without the involvement of school.

The whole-family context

So far, the discussion has focused on the significance of the parent–child relationship for children's development. These relationships are rightly seen as being of central importance, although it should be noted that, until relatively recently, mothers have been more studied than fathers. In order to fully appreciate their particular contribution, both mother–child and father–child relationships need to be viewed within the context of the multiple roles and inter-relationships within the family that make up the learning context of home. It is easier to observe and describe interactions between two people than the more subtle and indirect effects that come into play when three or more participants are present. It is perhaps not surprising, therefore, that traditionally the dyadic relationships within the family, for example mother–daughter or brother–sister, have been the focus of most research. However, increasing consideration has been given more recently to the impact of broader family dynamics. Figure 3.1 provides a simple illustration of this: the bi-directional arrows represent the reciprocal nature of the

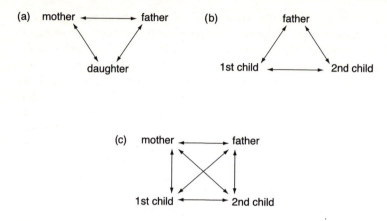

Figure 3.1 Examples of interactions between family relationships

interacting influences. Examples (a) and (b) indicate the ways in which the relationship between two family members both influences and is influenced by their separate relationships with a third. Thus, in the first example, the nature of the relationship between the mother and father affects the way in which each interacts with their child; and in the second example, the quality of the father's involvement with each of his children affects the development of the sibling relationship. Example (c) illustrates the degree of additional complexity which is introduced simply by considering the interacting influences of a fourth family member.

The network of multiple roles and relationships that many children experience within the family is far more intricate than illustrated in Figure 3.1. Add to this a recognition of the ways in which relationships evolve and change over time, and it becomes evident what a complex, demanding and powerful social context for learning families can represent.

The role that different family members play in supporting children's learning is clearly affected not only by the whole-family dynamics, but also by wider influences, including patterns of parental employment outside the home. However, mothers are usually the primary caregivers and, as such, undertake the majority of child rearing and domestic tasks. Fathers' roles tend to develop in ways that are complementary: for example, they may take on a more direct child care role with the first-born child following the birth of a sibling. Brannen and her colleagues (Brannen *et al.*, 2000) found that, while older children perceived similarities in parental roles, they often characterised their mothers as particularly associated with support at home, and their fathers as supporting their links to the outside world. Where there are siblings in the family, they also typically play a salient role. The relationship can be an ambivalent one, for feelings of sibling rivalry are not rare: Goodnow and Burns (1985), for example, reported an equal number of positive and negative comments made by children about their siblings. However, Dunn's research (e.g. Dunn, 1984, 1998) has demonstrated the significant contribution siblings can play in promoting social understanding, and Brannen et al. (2000) have described siblings fulfilling a wide range of positive roles, such as teachers, confidants and helpers. Among the other relatives who can play a significant part in family life, particular mention should be made of grandparents. Children often describe a close relationship with grandparents, who clearly contribute much to feelings of family continuity and belonging. The exact nature of the role that grandparents play obviously varies, depending on their age, how close by they live and their relationship with the children's parents, but it can include direct practical and emotional support. A sense of reciprocal care and concern can be highly developed among their grandchildren, who frequently refer to a desire to look after and help them.

Such reciprocity in children's relationships is not restricted to their grandparents, of course. Research studies cite examples of both practical help and what Brannen et al. (2000) term 'empathetic support' to their parents, siblings and others. The recognition of this reciprocity serves as a reminder that children themselves are key contributors to the learning context of home, where they are involved in ongoing negotiation of their relationships. Mayall's (2001) summary of how 9- and 10-year-olds in her research describe their family relationships captures the nature of their active involvement:

> They talk about their participant activity in structuring relationships, arguing, comforting and listening. Their accounts indicate their knowledge of adults' . . . feelings, motives and reasoning. They describe their participation in the complexities and conflicts involved in decision-making.
>
> (p. 127)

Tensions can obviously exist, for example with respect to perceptions of parental control and competing interests between different family members (Goodnow and Burns, 1985). Nevertheless, despite the unequal power relations that exist between adults and children, there are reciprocal interdependencies between them (Morrow, 1998; Punch, 2001), and at their most positive, families act as sources of mutual help and support.

Patterns of interdependence within families shift over time as both children and their parents grow older. Central to this shift is a gradual renegotiation of the parent–child relationship as children's independence and identity with their peer group increase. Typically, parental control strategies become less direct, and over time subtle readjustments take place with respect to rights, status and autonomy. There is obviously diversity in individual families' responses to the transitions that take place through adolescence to young adulthood. Reflecting the broader ecological influences on family life, as might be anticipated, their responses are also affected by gender, social class and cultural variables (Brannen, 1996). Particular issues can arise, too, for children with special educational needs and their families. These are highlighted in the following discussion.

Families and children with special educational needs

Much of the literature concerning families of children with special educational needs is based on research with those whose children have significant developmental delays or disabilities. Their children's needs have therefore typically been identified before formal schooling begins. In most respects, they resemble other families: they are subject to the same influences and demonstrate the same range of individual diversity. Nevertheless, there are also some distinctive aspects of parenting and family life that need to be acknowledged.

As Dale (1996) has observed, parents rarely expect that their children will have significant special needs, and therefore the identification of these often causes them to experience an intense emotional reaction, which can include complex feelings of shock, denial, anger, grief and anxiety. Their responses will be mediated by their understandings and beliefs concerning the nature of their children's needs. These in turn are likely to be influenced by their prior experiences and the attitudes of family and friends, as well as by broader societal and cultural perspectives on disability and difference. For some parents, emotional adjustment to their circumstances can be accompanied by continued periods of sorrow as well as by what Carpenter and Carpenter (1997) describe as the 'chronic vulnerability' arising from uncertainty about what to expect in the future. F. Russell (2003), who has considered parental expectations in detail, outlines the ways in which parents of disabled children need to rebuild and develop their expectations concerning their child, the nature of their parenting role and the range and quality of service provision. She argues that explicit attention to these developing expectations is essential to professional understanding of parental perspectives.

Parental beliefs and expectations change and develop over time, both influencing and influenced by their interactions with their children. When children have particular impairments, parents can find their responses unpredictable or difficult to read: this can impede the development of the sort of synchronised interactive sequences that have previously been described as typical of parent–infant 'dialogue'. It can also undermine parental feelings of confidence in their own interaction skills. Studies of parent–child interaction generally report that, by comparison with other parent–child pairs, developmentally delayed children tend to be more passive and less responsive, and their parents more directive (Beveridge, 1989). This may be because parents feel they need to provide a higher level of stimulation and structure to keep the dialogue going, particularly when their children are very young. It may also be associated with a tendency for parents of children with identified difficulties to engage in more explicit teaching activities in the pre-school years, as they are frequently encouraged to do so by professionals. Like any parents, they develop their own natural teaching strategies, and some are more effective than others in scaffolding their children's learning. However, many welcome reassurance and support, and in those cases where interactive difficulties persist, they may need more specific help with strategies for promoting their children's participation.

Depending on the nature of their needs, children's care requirements can be extensive and in some cases, parents will also require specific support for these, for example if they are expected to use specific therapy techniques at home. A further aspect of parenting that is heightened when children have particular needs has been characterised by Read (2000) as a mediation role. Mediation is sometimes required in a number of demanding contexts. For example, where their understanding is lacking and attitudes unhelpful, relatives and friends can become sources of stress rather than support. Parents may find, therefore, that they need to intercede, in order to help them appreciate the nature of their children's strengths and needs, and to promote positive expectations. Beyond their immediate circle there are also instances, sometimes arising from encounters in public places, when parents feel they have to explain and negotiate the situation both for their children and for the others involved. In addition, children with significant needs and disabilities tend to be involved with a wide range of different services, and the parental mediation role can extend to service providers as well. Parents often feel dependent on professionals for advice, particularly in the early stages when they are learning about the impact of their children's needs on parenting routines and interactions. However, they do not always consider that they have been helped to care for their children in the way that felt right for them:

> A child's upbringing may become professionalised, with mothers under considerable pressure to do the 'right' thing in the 'right' way according to the professional edicts of the time.
>
> (Read, 2000: 108)

As parents develop their knowledge and beliefs concerning the best ways of meeting their children's needs, they may become more confident intermediaries on behalf of their children and less dependent on professional judgements.

Read's research focused on mothers, and it is they who usually undertake not only the primary care activities at home, but also the major liaison role with service providers. As previously discussed, parents tend to develop their roles and relationships within the family in complementary ways. However, Carpenter and Herbert (1997) caution that in their dealings with mothers, professionals may unwittingly contribute to a perception of fathers as peripheral, and thereby add to the pressure on both parents. They observe that when fathers feel left out of the process of information exchange and decision-making with professionals, this can lead to their taking a less participant role than they would wish in relation to the services their children receive. With this in mind, it is salutary to reflect that, among all the well-documented sources of stress on parents of disabled children – social, emotional, practical, financial – they often describe dealing with professionals as the most stressful (Beresford, 1995).

Linked to the mediation role, is parental advocacy. Most parents are likely to advocate on their children's behalf at some point. However, for parents whose children have special educational needs, the significance of their advocacy is heightened because of the risks of marginalisation that they face. One parent has described the experience as follows:

'If you have a child who is not labelled by your society, then no one expects you to have to go out into the community and argue for access to the same resources in health, education, and welfare provisions that other children have as a right of citizenship. Yet for parents of a child with a disability, advocacy becomes necessary because we suddenly confront a society that is often willing to discriminate on the basis of disability. Many families share similar experiences of advocacy struggles for their children.'

(Brown, 1999: 29)

Ideally, as their children grow older, parents will increasingly support them in advocating for themselves too. It was noted earlier that some parents may require help in developing their children's initiations and active participation in interactions: they may equally need support if they are to facilitate a transition towards greater autonomy and self-advocacy. There is a tension for all parents between keeping their children safe and secure and promoting their independence. This tension is accentuated when children's needs make them particularly vulnerable. In such cases, direct parental monitoring of activities tends to be maintained to a later age. This is particularly likely in situations where, because of separate schooling, their children are isolated from the sort of local peer group that might support them in activities beyond the home and family setting. Transition through adolescence to young adulthood can therefore be 'a complex and difficult time' (Dee, 2000: 142) from the perspectives of both the parents and their children.

The focus of the preceding discussion has been on the parental role in relation to children who have developmental difficulties or disabilities. In concluding this section, reference should also be made to their siblings. Parents often express particular concern about their response to having a brother or sister with special needs, and are anxious to minimise the likelihood of potentially negative effects. There is a balance to be sought between ensuring that children are alert to their sibling's needs, yet ensuring that this knowledge does not put them under undue pressure. Research studies tend to demonstrate that, as with any siblings, some of their relationships are more positive than others, and that feelings of ambivalence are not uncommon. Some siblings seem to wish to take on an actively supportive and responsible role whereas others seek to avoid this. On the whole, individual diversity in response is associated with a number of interacting factors, including the age difference with their sibling, parental expectations, their own temperament and the extent to which they feel they are an equally important focus of their parents' attention. Like other family members, they frequently express the need for information about the nature of their sibling's needs and, where they have concerns about this or about perceived expectations of their role, they also need support and understanding (Meyer and Vadasy, 1997).

Family contexts for learning: aspects of diversity

This chapter has emphasised the significance of the family, with its close affective and reciprocal relationships, as a primary context for children's learning. The experience of progressively more demanding activities and interactions at home lays the foundations for subsequent developmental transitions, for example to peer groups (Parke *et al.*, 1994; Mize *et al.*, 1998) as well as to schools. The consensus of research in this area is that children's positive social, emotional and cognitive growth is associated with their active participation in home environments that are warm, stimulating and responsive (e.g. Pugh *et al.*, 1994; Meadows, 1996; Sylva *et al.*, 2003). In characterising the nature of home learning environments, discussion so far has been primarily concerned with common patterns and with the particular issues that can become heightened when children have special educational needs. Throughout, though, mention has also been made of individual variation between families: Box 3.1 summarises the main aspects of diversity which have been referred to. This is not an exhaustive list, but rather an illustration of the interacting dimensions of difference in family life that children experience.

It is clearly the case that the parental contribution to the quality of home learning environments is a significant one, and equally clearly, that parents vary in the personal resources they bring to their role. For example, their knowledge and understanding of child development, their communicative skills and their educational aspirations for their children are all likely to influence not only the

---

Box 3.1 Interacting dimensions of difference in family life

Whole-family context	e.g. family structure and membership
	roles and relationships
	parental employment
	times of transition
Parental variables	e.g. beliefs, expectations
	confidence
	interactive strategies
	explicit teaching
	mediation and advocacy
Child variables	e.g. responsiveness
	predictability
	special educational needs
	disability
Broader influences	e.g. contacts with professionals
	socio-economic and cultural variables.

---

nature of their parent–child interactions, but also their relationships with schools and other services. However, it is important to recognise that parents' personal resources interact with the other dimensions of family diversity that are illustrated in Box 3.1. Thus, for example, differing family structures and relationships offer differing levels of support for parents. Cultural variation in beliefs, values and practices with respect to child rearing also impacts on the parental role. Further, some children's characteristics, such as those that are associated with a lack of responsiveness, unpredictability, special educational needs or disability, heighten the demands made of their parents.

Broader stresses upon parental and family functioning can take social, material and financial forms. As will be discussed in Chapter 4, the learning environment of home is clearly affected by poverty and overcrowding, and where families have pressing demands arising from financial hardship and poor housing, involvement with their children's schools may not be among parents' first priorities. Socio-economic and minority ethnic status interact together for some families, and where this is so, the effects of poverty on parental take-up of services can be further compounded by a lack of confidence, familiarity and knowledge concerning service provision.

The extent of parental resilience to additional stresses and demands is affected by personal qualities such as confidence and self-esteem, and by evolving relationships within the family. It will also be influenced in part by the nature of the support available beyond the family. Although parents can feel supported by individual professionals with whom they come into contact, contacts with services can also add to family stress. Balancing the demands of child care, employment, domestic commitments, liaison with schools and with other services, can be difficult for any parent, and systems for parent–professional liaison are rarely set up with the degree of flexibility necessary to respond to a wide range of differing family circumstances.

A recognition of these interacting dimensions of variation between families has clear implications for schools, if they are to seek to build upon the learning experiences of home and promote inclusive educational practice. At a whole-school level, for example, arrangements for communication with parents need to be sufficiently flexible that they do not create unnecessary barriers for lone parents, working parents and parents whose spoken or written English skills are limited. If home–school communication is to include all parents, this requires constructive attitudes towards family diversity on the part of individual teachers. It is not unusual for teachers to judge parents on the basis of their children's learning and behaviour at school and to draw the inference that particular home backgrounds are educationally deficient in some way. In order to combat these and other unhelpful assumptions, they require an informed understanding of the complex nature of interacting influences on children's learning at home. They also need to be alert to the relationship between home learning and the formal educational experiences offered at school, and to recognise the ways in which school-based learning represents a significant departure from children's experiences of home. Hannon (1995), for example, has highlighted relevant features of home learning as being spontaneous and flexible; shaped by children's interests; and based on close, but varied family relationships with those of differing ages. By contrast, he describes school learning as being planned and timetabled; shaped by the formal curriculum; and taking place with the learner in a single age group and in a single role characterised by a formal relationship with the teacher. The gap between the learning demands of home and school that Hannon describes is present for all children. Indeed, it can be argued that it plays an essential part in their education, because it serves to promote and extend their thinking and knowledge in new ways (Tizard and Hughes, 1984). However, there is no doubt that the disjunction between the worlds of home and school is more extensive for some children than for others, and further, that the degree of adaptation required can place them at a significant disadvantage by comparison with their peers. Parental, school-based and wider community initiatives that aim to minimise the risk of such educational disadvantage form the focus of the next chapter.

Chapter 4

Educational disadvantage and the home–school relationship

The focus of this chapter is on educational disadvantage and the sorts of strategies that have been developed to try to counteract it. Particular consideration is given to the significance of the home–school relationship. Educational disadvantage is a complex and multifaceted phenomenon, which incorporates socio-cultural and economic as well as educational dimensions. Dyson (1997), for example, has observed that many of the educational difficulties that children demonstrate in school, such as disaffection, disruption and underachievement, are associated with patterns of social disadvantage and the associated stresses on families and children. Further, it is well-established that there is a clear link between parental socio-economic status and a large range of mild to moderate learning difficulties and social, emotional and behavioural difficulties that are identified among children with special educational needs (e.g. Croll, 2002).

An exploration of the potential impact of family poverty on children's educational prospects helps to illuminate the complexity of the interacting factors that may be involved. Poverty affects all aspects of life, including housing, nutrition and health, as well as education:

> Having no money and living below the official poverty line affects every other aspect of living. It causes immense stress and worry to parents and carers, leaving them little time to enjoy their children, far less co-operate with schools in promoting their children's learning. It has a major effect on nutrition and general health and therefore heightens vulnerability to illness and accidents. It is nearly always linked to sub-standard

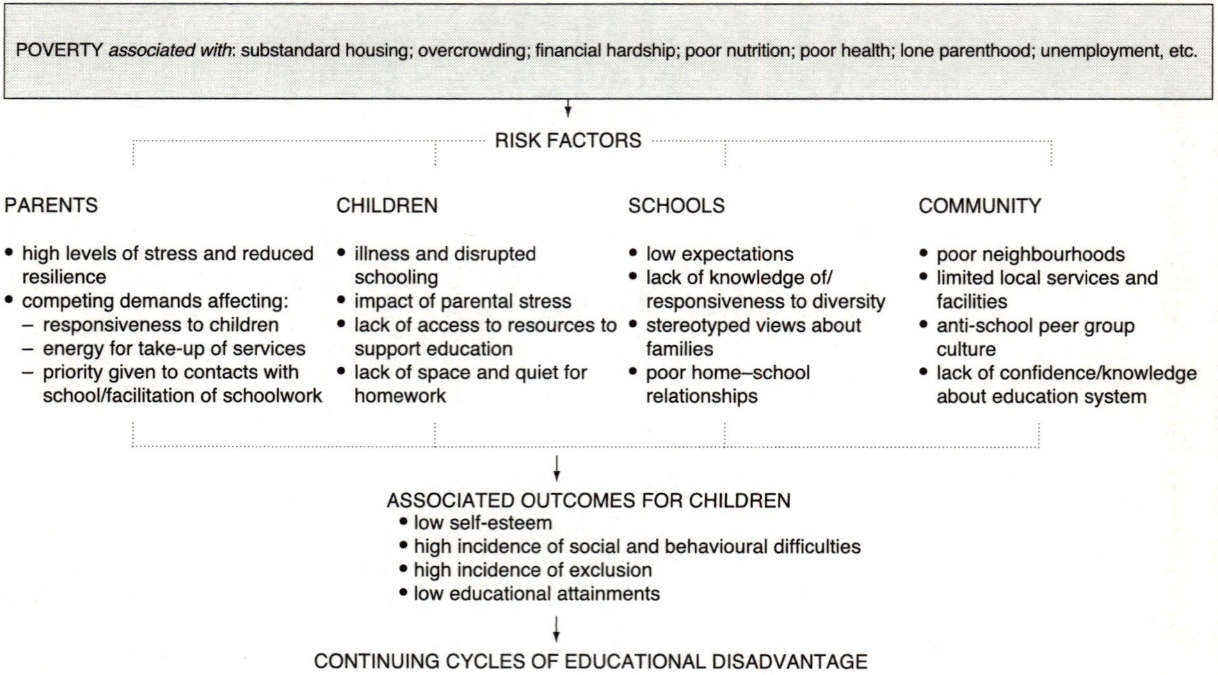

| POVERTY *associated with*: substandard housing; overcrowding; financial hardship; poor nutrition; poor health; lone parenthood; unemployment, etc. |

RISK FACTORS

PARENTS	CHILDREN	SCHOOLS	COMMUNITY
• high levels of stress and reduced resilience • competing demands affecting: – responsiveness to children – energy for take-up of services – priority given to contacts with school/facilitation of schoolwork	• illness and disrupted schooling • impact of parental stress • lack of access to resources to support education • lack of space and quiet for homework	• low expectations • lack of knowledge of/responsiveness to diversity • stereotyped views about families • poor home–school relationships	• poor neighbourhoods • limited local services and facilities • anti-school peer group culture • lack of confidence/knowledge about education system

ASSOCIATED OUTCOMES FOR CHILDREN
• low self-esteem
• high incidence of social and behavioural difficulties
• high incidence of exclusion
• low educational attainments

CONTINUING CYCLES OF EDUCATIONAL DISADVANTAGE

Figure 4.1 Educational disadvantage: an illustration of risk factors associated with poverty

housing and to overcrowding, which in turn makes it difficult
for children to find a quiet corner.

(Mittler, 2000: 49)

Figure 4.1 draws on the work of a number of authors (McGurk and
Soriano, 1998; Chazan, 2000; Cox, 2000; Gersch *et al.*, 2000; Mittler,
2000; Palmer *et al.*, 2003) to illustrate some of the indicative risk
factors that can be specifically related to education and educational
outcomes. It identifies possible disadvantages arising within the
home, school and local community contexts, and from the interaction between these. At home, for example, when parents experience high levels of stress, this is likely to reduce their resilience in
dealing with the competing demands they face. Accordingly, their
stress may impact not only on their interactions with their children
but also on their dealings with educational and related services.
In addition to their experiences of parental stress, children living
in poverty may also be affected by illness and disrupted schooling.
Where limited financial resources restrict access to resources to
support their schoolwork, such as books and trips, or the space
and quiet to study at home, this poses further barriers to successful
learning.

Moving beyond the family context to the community within
which they live, there may be a generalised lack of confidence and
knowledge concerning the education system, and a shared sense of
lowered expectations about contacts with school. Further, in poor
or rundown neighbourhoods there are often limited local services
and facilities to support children's learning both in and out of
school. An anti-school peer group culture can thrive when school
relationships are poorly developed, and it is evident that the peer
group is likely to become particularly influential for children in
situations where their parents are preoccupied by financial and
other stressors. Risk factors are not only associated with home
and local community, however, but also with school. For example,
teachers working in schools that serve poor communities may lack
knowledge of and responsiveness to the diversity of home circumstances that children experience, and they may hold stereotyped
views of families. Factors such as these, in interaction with child,
family and community stresses, have a negative impact on teacher
expectations of children and on the quality of home–school relationships, both of which play a significant role in relation to educational outcomes.

Of course, not all children living in poverty experience all of these potential risks. There is individual diversity among parents in their resilience and resourcefulness in dealing with the stresses of chronic financial hardship, and some community neighbourhoods are characterised by more supportive networks than others. Importantly, both individual teachers and whole-school staffs also demonstrate marked differences in the effectiveness of their practices (Reynolds, 1995). It is generally acknowledged that the support of one or more close and continuing positive relationships can act to bolster children's resilience in dealing with stresses, and many children appear able to cope with one source of stress in their lives. However, the more risks they face in home, school and local community, the more likely it is that the cumulative effects will lead to significant educational difficulties. As indicated in Figure 4.1, associated outcomes can include low self-esteem and poor social and academic achievements. Further, where children's experiences of school have been negative, they may find it difficult to communicate with and develop positive relationships with their own children's teachers when they themselves become parents. This highlights just one of the many possible ways in which poor educational experience can contribute to a continuing cycle of educational disadvantage.

In addition to poverty, minority ethnic status can also be associated with educational disadvantage. Although there is evidence that schools have become better at responding to ethnic diversity than was previously the case, there remains a disproportionate representation of particular minority ethnic groups among children identified as having special educational needs (Tomlinson, 2000) and among those formally excluded from school (Wright *et al.*, 2000; Palmer *et al.*, 2003). Obvious barriers to home–school communication arise for parents who lack fluency in the English language as well as confidence in their interactions with staff. Further obstacles can result when parents are unfamiliar with the school system. For their part, teachers can lack knowledge concerning cultural and religious diversity and can make unfounded assumptions about family life (Bastiani,1997). As a result, the potential for discrepancy between home and school expectations regarding formal education that is present for any child becomes heightened, and this can lead to difficulties in establishing constructive parent–teacher relationships. It should be noted, too, that where minority ethnic families live in socially and economically deprived circumstances, this will compound the risk of educational disadvantage for their children.

While a broad range of generalised difficulties in learning and behaviour are associated with parental socio-economic status, this association does not apply with respect to disability. Nevertheless, the potential barriers to learning that exist at home and school and in wider community contexts are such that disabled children almost inevitably experience educational disadvantage. This disadvantage is further accentuated in interaction with social class variables (Evans and Vincent, 1997) and minority ethnic status (Diniz, 1997; Chamba *et al.*, 1999). Distinctions can be drawn between specific aspects of the experience of disabled children and those whose needs are perceived to stem more clearly from social and economic factors. Nevertheless, as will be seen from the following discussion, there are also similarities in the policy initiatives that have been developed to try to overcome the obstacles to their educational success.

Although a multiplicity of interacting factors can be identified that contribute to educational disadvantage, it should be acknowledged that this does not lead to any simple explanation for the processes through which risk factors operate, nor of the steps that might be taken to prevent this from happening (Mittler, 2000). What is apparent, though, is that policies that aim to counteract disadvantage must themselves be multifaceted and go far beyond a purely educational focus. Three themes can be highlighted which underpin current approaches: these emphasise the significance of parental coping strategies; community contexts, and the home–school–community relationship. The first of these has traditionally received most attention, and has led to initiatives that have two interacting component parts: parent education aimed at enhancing parenting skills and direct early intervention work with children.

Parental coping strategies: parent education and early intervention

In recognition of the primary role that parents play in children's development and learning, it has been argued that support should be offered directly to parents in ways that enhance their resilience and hence the quality of their parenting. From this perspective, parent education has the potential to act as a protective factor against educational disadvantage (McGurk and Soriano, 1998; Pugh *et al.*, 1994; Sylva *et al.*, 2003).

In the past, traditional approaches to parent education were based on simplistic explanations of disadvantage. That is, because children from poorer homes did less well at school than their peers, their parents' child rearing strategies were assumed to be deficient in some way. Accordingly the professional task was seen to be to compensate for this by directing parents in approved ways of interacting with their children and managing their behaviour. However, such deficit notions of parenting were contested by an accumulation of research evidence (e.g. Wells, 1983; Tizard and Hughes, 1984; Pellegrini and Galda, 1998) which demonstrated that, while there might be differences in style between parents from differing social and cultural backgrounds, most were competent facilitators of their children's learning, and assumptions of cognitive and linguistic deprivation were not supported by empirical evidence. As a result, it became increasingly recognised that there are diverse approaches to successful parenting, and that the role of parent education should primarily be to help parents become more confident and skilled in their own strategies for bringing up their children.

While parent education programmes take different forms, they tend to include information, advice and opportunities for sharing and reflection upon experiences with a group of other parents. They seek to help parents understand both their own needs and those of their children, with the aim of enhancing the parent–child relationship (Pugh *et al.*, 1994; Wolfendale and Einzig, 1999). In some cases for specific groups, such as parents of children with developmental delays and disabilities or problematic behaviour, they also include the learning of specific skills. Ball (1998), for example, has reported that approximately 80 per cent of local education authorities have Portage services for young preschool children with special educational needs. This individual and home-based service relies on parents as the primary teachers of their own children: short-term learning targets are agreed by parents and Portage workers during regular home visits, and parents are encouraged to adopt particular strategies for teaching these. Evidence has been built up over more than twenty years that parents are fully capable of successfully achieving such specific objectives with their children, and the Portage approach has proved to be a robust and flexible service model (White, 1997).

A number of criticisms have been raised about parent education programmes, however. When they are targeted at parents of children deemed at risk of educational difficulty, there are obvious concerns about the extent to which they are seen as stigmatising families. There is a certain irony in seeking to prevent disadvantage and exclusion through means that are themselves potentially exclusionary, and for this reason it is often argued that the programmes should be made available for all parents (Einzig, 1999). Another cause of concern is the extent to which, as a strategy, parent education focuses attention on individuals rather than on the institutions and social processes that contribute to educational disadvantage (Power, 2001). This can serve to put an onus on families in a way that distracts attention from the wider constraints under which they operate. Within the family itself, programmes are typically directed to one parent (usually the mother) rather than taking account of whole-family dynamics. Moreover, despite evident caution in most programmes against an attempt to tell parents how they should bring up their children, there remains the possibility that subtle messages may be given about conforming to practices that do not take account of significant aspects of family diversity (Vincent, 2000).

Additional concerns are specific to cases where a formalised parental teaching role is emphasised. While many parents teach their own child successfully, not all are able to do so. Some may not see explicit teaching as a significant part of their role, and care is needed to ensure that undue emphasis on this does not appear to devalue other aspects of their parenting. Some, because of other pressing priorities, may not be able to undertake as much teaching as they would wish. There is a risk too that parents may start to feel wholly responsible for their children's learning and behaviour and experience emotions of guilt and anxiety that they should be doing more, particularly in situations where their children's progress is slow or inconsistent. Equally important is the concern that a focus on specific techniques and methods can result in parents feeling de-skilled and dependent on professional judgement in order to establish 'correct' ways of teaching their children.

Despite these concerns, though, it is important to acknowledge that those parents who have attended parent education programmes are generally reported to feel positively about what they have gained from their participation (Grimshaw and McGuire, 1998; Vincent, 2000), and it is not unusual for parents who have received the Portage service, for example, to go on to become Portage workers themselves. It should be noted too that, in recent years, those work-ing in the field of parent education have endeavoured to address the criticisms that were levelled at earlier practice, by developing approaches that are more parent-led and responsive to cultural and family diversity. In an attempt to move beyond potentially stig-matising interventions, Hinton (1999) has described a life cycle approach to parenting support, which is directed at predictable times of uncertainty and transition (such as the early years, transi-tion to school, adolescence, and so on), and is open to all parents rather than only those whose children are deemed to be at risk of educational difficulties. Ball (1998), too, has argued that parenting support should not end once a child starts school. However, as a strategy for combating educational disadvantage, parenting edu-cation continues to be targeted primarily on parents of preschool children who are judged to be at risk because of family circum-stances or identified developmental difficulties and disabilities. Typically also combined with direct professional work with the children, this form of early intervention has been described in national policy as 'the best way to tackle educational disadvantage' (DfEE, 1997a: 12).

Mitchell and Brown (1991) have described a general consensus among those working in early intervention that, through support of both parents and children, their aims are to provide early stimu-lation as a basis for subsequent learning; to minimise existing diffi-culties; and to try to prevent later difficulties from arising. Thus, the notion of a child being 'at risk' of going on to experience subse-quent difficulties is central to the development of early intervention strategies. As Cox (2000) has observed, this notion carries with it the possibility of a negative effect on expectations, and therefore there is a real need for high-quality provision linked to realistically high expectations in order to ensure that the potential benefits of intervention are realised.

Evidence for the effectiveness of early intervention derives for the most part from research that has been undertaken over an extensive period of time into the impact of the Head Start preschool initiative in the United States. Lazar and his colleagues, for example, under-took a detailed analysis of the long-term effects of the early inter-vention programmes that they judged to be of the highest quality (Lazar and Darlington, 1983; Lazar, 1985). The most successful were those that provided multi-agency services for parents as well as for children, and included home visiting and direct parental involvement in educational interventions. The researchers found that, during their schooling, children who had been involved in these programmes were less likely than comparable groups to be held back a grade or to be referred to special education classes. They 'perceived themselves more positively, were more achievement oriented, and had more realistic vocational aspirations' (Lazar, 1985: 30), and after school, they were more likely to attend further education and to gain employment. Evaluation of the Perry Pre-school Project (Berrueta-Clement *et al.*, 1984) has detailed similarly positive outcomes lasting into young adulthood, with less likelihood of criminal activity and better social adjustment being reported. In her review of research in this area, Sylva (2000) highlights the significance of the frequently reported finding that early intervention has an effect not only on academic attainment, but also on personal and motivational development. She argues that there is evidence of a positive impact on what she characterises as social commitment, with programme participants going on to demonstrate greater engagement and identification not only at school but also within the broader community in which they live. Although questions might be raised about the generalisability of these findings to other country contexts, Sylva and her colleagues have recently reported UK evidence that is consistent with the premise that good-quality preschool education, in which educational aims are shared with parents, enhances the chances of educational success for socially disadvantaged children when they reach primary school (Sylva *et al.*, 2003).

The government has demonstrated its confidence in the potential effectiveness of early intervention by making this central to its strategy for both preventing and responding to a wide range of children's needs (DfES, 2003b, 2004). Foremost among its current initiatives is the Sure Start programme for children under 4 years old and their families. This 'aims to improve the life chances of younger children through better access to early education and play, health services for children and parents, family support and advice on nurturing' (Glass, 1999: 257). Drawing on the longitudinal evaluations from the United States that were described previously, it has as an explicit purpose the attempt to promote children's preschool development, so that they are ready to thrive when they enter formal schooling, but also seeks to achieve long-term effects with respect to their subsequent educational performance, employment and social inclusion. Importantly, as discussed shortly, it is also informed by the recognition that, to be effective, programmes need to be rooted in local communities and responsive to social and cultural diversity.

Community contexts

In an influential review of the first Head Start programmes, Bronfenbrenner (1976) drew attention to the fact that the most disadvantaged children and families were not served well by traditional approaches to early intervention. Their take-up of the services offered was comparatively low, and those who did participate showed fewer benefits than other families. Bronfenbrenner argued, therefore, that what was required was an ecological approach, involving coordinated multi-agency provision that was sufficiently flexible to adapt to local community contexts. This implies the need not only to support individuals, but also to find ways of enhancing community confidence and networks of mutual support. The Sure Start initiative explicitly attempts to do this, by encouraging the use of other local resources and providing opportunities for parents and other members of the community to become involved in the planning, management and delivery of services. As a result of this locally driven approach, Jack and Jordan (1999) argue that the best of the Sure Start services play an important part in strengthening the community:

> They provide opportunities for mutual social support and reciprocal relationships to develop between parents, as well as enabling volunteer helpers and professional workers to provide the sort of information and emotional support which can be a crucial ingredient in improving parent–child interactions and developmental outcomes for children. . . . The best projects also explicitly attempt to assist parents to make more use of other community resources and encourage them to go on to become providers of the service in their own turn. In all of these ways, it can be seen that such services are playing a part in developing the social capital of the communities in which they are operating.
>
> (Jack and Jordan, 1999: 248)

The Sure Start programme is aimed at the 25 per cent of neighbourhoods that are judged to be the most socially deprived. There can be drawbacks in targeting disadvantaged communities in this way, and concerns have been expressed about the extent to which both Sure Start and other early intervention initiatives reach all the families who would benefit from them. There are considerations too about the location of specific resources in areas where there is a concentration of impoverished families: for example, Sylva and her colleagues found in their research that disadvantaged children benefit most from preschool provision in settings where there is an inclusive mix of children from different social backgrounds (Sylva *et al.*, 2003). These and other questions are likely to be addressed by the national evaluation team which is currently studying the impact of the programme. They are focusing their investigation not only on the nature of its effects on children, families and communities, but also on identifying the conditions that are most associated with effectiveness (NESS (National Evaluation of Sure Start) Research Team, 2004).

An emphasis on early intervention as a strategy for combating educational disadvantage can be criticised when it is seen to lead to a narrow focus on 'getting the child ready for school' (Grant and Williams, 2000: 238), because this can serve to distract attention from the important role that schools themselves have to play. In parallel with early intervention policies, therefore, there is a need for school-based initiatives that have a strong community dimension.

Home–school–community links

Parent education and early intervention approaches have directed attention towards parents and their children's learning experiences at home. The once prevalent notions of linguistic and cognitive deprivation among families living in disadvantaged circumstances have been largely discredited, and as a result, approaches are informed by a greater recognition of what all families contribute to their children's learning. Nevertheless, as Davie (2000) has argued, a respect for family diversity should not prevent acknowledgement of the real difficulties that can result for children whose learning experiences in home and local community are furthest removed from the assumptions and values they encounter at school. If such disadvantages are to be overcome, this necessitates strategies that focus on schools as well as families.

The principle that strong links between home, school and community represent a powerful means for overcoming educational disadvantage is fundamental to the community education tradition. This tradition takes as its starting point the need to acknowledge that there are potential barriers to home–school links to be overcome, and that these require schools to develop strategies that make them more accessible and responsive to the local communities that they serve. The approach involves a commitment to community development and empowerment, underpinned by an explicit attempt to take account of and demonstrate respect for the concerns, priorities and needs of the community. From this perspective, school is viewed as an inclusive learning facility which offers both children and their families the opportunity to develop relevant skills and knowledge (Watt, 1989; Ball, 1998). It is essential to the nature of a community-based approach that it should be adapted to local circumstances and requirements, but common features of the provision made by community education schools typically include shared neighbourhood facilities, a community-oriented curriculum, and participation in school activities, decision-making and management by parents and other members of the local community.

Although less well-established than its early intervention policies, the government does have in place initiatives that can be regarded as following in the community education tradition, in that they are based on the premise that schools can become central resources for their local neighbourhoods. In particular, it proposes that, by 2006, all local education authorities will have at least one 'extended school' (DfES, 2003b). Schools that are so designated are intended to be open beyond usual school hours in order to make extended educational provision for pupils, families and other members of the community, through operating in partnership with other local services and voluntary organisations. Although the exact range of services provided is expected to be tailored to reflect the requirements of the local community, it is likely to include study support, child care and family and adult learning. Extended schools will also bring together health and social care services on site.

Dyson and Robson (1999) argue that there has been more ideological debate than evaluative research into the effectiveness of community education, and further, they observe that in practice there is little opportunity for local communities to become engaged in decision-making processes in schools. Similarly, Crowther *et al.* (2003) question the extent to which schools have the capacity to make a significant contribution to the local community. However, although there may have been slow progress in the development of community education approaches, Ball (1998) has identified a number of community and family links that schools do typically adopt to varying degrees. She includes the following in her typology of school–family–community links: home–school communication; encouragement of learning activities at home; family and community help for schools; school support for families; parental and community participation in school management; and collaboration between schools and community agencies. She highlights the potential benefits for children, parents and schools of an approach based on community education principles, and on the basis of her review of school practice, she provides support for the view that effective links of this nature can play a key part in combating underachievement and disadvantage.

Home, school and educational disadvantage

An examination of the complex interacting influences that contribute to educational disadvantage inevitably involves a consideration of the roles of families and schools and the relationship between them. Home and school make different demands of children, for as Tizard and Hughes (1984: 263) have observed: 'The learning experiences, the discipline, the communication requirements, the physical and social environments of these worlds are very different'. These differing demands are potentially constructive, because children need to develop the knowledge and skills that enable them to learn from diverse experiences in a wide range of social contexts. In order to do this successfully, though, they must be able to build on and extend their home-based learning at school. By contrast, when they face a fragmentation between the learning experiences of home and school, this puts them at a significant disadvantage by comparison with their peers. For this reason, policy initiatives that attempt to counteract educational disadvantage have sought to bridge the gap between home and school.

Extensive attention has focused on the early learning context of home, where the aim has been to enhance the early development of children who are judged to be at risk of educational difficulties. The interrelated strategies of parent education and early intervention have been developed with the intention of providing these children with 'a head start' for when they begin school. However, these strategies cannot stand alone, but must be complemented by directing equal attention to the development of school-focused strategies that are responsive to the diversity of children's learning experiences at home and in their local community. As Norwich (1998) has argued, there is a need to distinguish between the sorts of educational need that may be prevented by the provision of high-quality early intervention and family support, and those that will require continuing attention and special support throughout the school years. While not denying the significance of the structural and economic inequalities in society which are associated with educational disadvantage, the school role is therefore a vital one. Schools differ in the extent to which they promote effective inclusive practices that are supportive of children from diverse backgrounds and with diverse needs. A key to the improvement of their practice lies in the quality of the links they develop with other agencies and members of the local community and, most importantly, in the nature of the relationships they establish with their pupils and their pupils' parents. The promotion of positive home–school liaison is the subject of the next chapter.

Chapter 5

Developing home–school relationships

The development of positive home–school relationships is important for the education of all children. For the vast majority, home is their primary learning environment and therefore, as Bronfenbrenner's ecological model (1977) suggests, the nature of the transition from home-based learning to the expectations and demands of formal schooling is vitally important for children's subsequent educational progress. The successfulness with which children make this transition is enhanced when there are clear channels for constructive communication between home and school. Further, it is essential that communication between parents and teachers is two-way, in order to ensure not only that children's learning at home is built upon and developed at school, but also that their school learning is in turn consolidated and extended in out-of-school activities. Educational legislation has given due recognition to the rights that parents have with respect to information from and consultation with their children's schools, as outlined in Chapter 2. In parallel with these formal policy requirements, however, there has also been an increasing acknowledgement that schools need parental collaboration if teachers are to be fully effective in their educational role. This developing understanding of the significance of the home–school relationship has been supported by an accumulation of research evidence that demonstrates the positive effects on children's achievements and behaviour when their parents are actively involved in their education. Put simply, children are found to do better personally, socially and academically at school when their parents and teachers cooperate with each other. As a result, good home–school relationships have been identified as being central to school effectiveness and school improvement (Coleman, 1998; Wolfendale and Bastiani, 2000).

The importance of parental involvement in their children's education has been articulated particularly strongly in the case of children with special educational needs, whether their needs are related to social and economic disadvantage or to disability or to some combination of both. Children's needs cannot be seen in isolation from family structures and processes, nor from the wider factors that impact upon home life. It was emphasised in the previous chapter, for example, that the gap between home and school is particularly marked for children from disadvantaged home backgrounds, and that there is therefore a need for schools to find ways of supporting their learning by building family and community links. When their children are disabled, parents frequently acquire the sorts of specialist knowledge and understanding of the nature and implications of their impairment that are invaluable to schools in informing their teaching approach. Many parents will not only wish to contribute their own knowledge to schools, but may at the same time seek reassurance or guidance from schools concerning strategies at home. For all children with special educational needs, discontinuities in their learning experiences are potentially problematic, and therefore their educational experiences will be significantly more successful when there is agreement between their teachers and parents concerning educational goals and how best to achieve these. It should be noted, too, that children with special educational needs can make great demands on those responsible for their care, and that where this is so, both parents and teachers require support from each other in order to best fulfil their roles.

Bailey (1998: 177) has argued that:

> If a child is to be fully included in the life of a school, parents should be fully included as well. Parents should be equal partners in the process of schooling, fully involved in all the decisions the school makes about the child. They should feel confident that they can place their child in school without fear of exclusion because the child is different or difficult . . . they should also be regarded by the school system as needing additional support to help them cope with the problems and additional stresses presented by their children.

In these words, Bailey highlights the concern that, unless schools take steps to prevent this, it is not only children with special educational needs but also their parents who can be marginalised and experience discrimination. In doing so he provides a useful reminder that parental involvement is crucial to successful inclusive educational practice, and that an inclusive school is one that demonstrates that it values all members of the learning community, among whom must be counted parents as well as their children.

There is a varied range of ways in which schools can seek to involve parents, both individually and collectively, in order to build constructive relationships. Whatever form it takes, though, parental involvement must be underpinned by genuine two-way communication if it is to be successful. This chapter therefore begins with a consideration of the attitudes, commitment and skills that are required to promote effective parent–teacher communication. It then goes on to focus on the involvement of parents in a school's assessment, decision-making and review procedures; and active parent–teacher collaboration in teaching and behaviour management strategies.

Communication between home and school

Genuine two-way communication between home and school requires positive attitudes and commitment from both parents and teachers. A number of researchers (e.g. Croll and Moses, 1985, 2000; Galloway *et al.*, 1994; Kasama and Tett, 2001) have reported that teachers and other educational professionals can be quick to attribute difficulties at school to problems arising from home, and to make assumptions about the quality of parental support for their children's education. Parents are typically well aware of these assumptions, and this has an obvious impact on their attitude towards communication and cooperation with school. Where their children have special educational needs, they are also highly sensitised to any expression of negative attitudes among school staff concerning their difficulties or disability (Dale, 1996). It is inevitable that parents will feel more positive about their contacts with schools when they feel respected in their own right as parents, and equally importantly, when they perceive that their child is a positively valued member of the school. Hence the nature of a school's ethos and the quality of teacher–pupil relationships have clear implications for the sorts of relationships that are developed with parents.

Some parents become involved in the life of the school as a whole, for example through participating in parents' associations and extra-curricular activities or acting as parent governors. However, for all parents, their involvement with the school is first and foremost rooted in their concerns for their own children. Accordingly, their needs for communication from school typically centre on their hopes that their children will be happy and thrive, making good progress in their learning and achieving to the best of their ability. The sorts of information that parents say they want from schools therefore focus on the curriculum, including teaching approaches and organisational strategies; and on progress, achievements and any difficulties that their children are experiencing (Bastiani, 1992). To a large extent, this parental agenda for communication coincides with the policy requirements on provision of information that are required of schools as outlined in Chapter 2. However, parents also wish to ensure that school staff hold realistically high expectations of their children, and that these expectations are informed by an understanding of and responsiveness to their individual personal and social as well as their academic needs (Coleman, 1998). This necessitates that schools go beyond governmental policy requirements in their interactions with parents, towards a form of communication based on a commitment to a genuine sharing of information. It requires staff to acknowledge the distinctive knowledge and experience of parents, and to recognise the complementary roles that parents and teachers play in the promotion of children's learning. Further, it implies the need for teachers to develop the skills, confidence and sensitivity to the parental perspective that will enable them not only to provide clear, honest and accurate information concerning their children's learning and behaviour at school, but also to elicit and respond to parents' own in-depth knowledge, perspectives and insights.

Where children have special educational needs, the need for staff to develop an informed understanding and skills that will support positive communication with parents is heightened. The more knowledgeable that teachers are about the nature of children's strengths and difficulties, the better able they will be to communicate concerns and discuss possible strategies in a constructive and supportive way. There are frequently sensitive issues to discuss, and it is essential that both parents and teachers feel confident to express their own views. Some parents of children with special educational needs will seek support to think through their own concerns regarding their children, and to develop strategies that will help them deal with these. Where teachers aim to provide such support, Hornby (Hornby 1994, 2000; Hornby *et al.*, 1995) has argued that they need to extend their communication skills in ways associated with counselling, for example through the development of active listening and joint problem-solving techniques. Hornby also highlights the significance of the sort of skilled assertiveness that allows teachers to be both direct and diplomatic in their interactions with parents, and to respond constructively to disagreements and criticism when these occur.

Equally important as their communication skills, are the attitudes and commitment of teachers to the development of their relationships with parents. In one study of home–school communication (Beveridge, 1997), special educational needs coordinators (SENCOs) have emphasised the need to make themselves available and approachable, explaining for example that 'I want parents to feel OK about coming in and I do a lot of work to try to encourage them to do that' (ibid., p. 64). It is apparent from their responses that the parents in this study were appreciative of staff who adopted such an approach. Typical parental comments include: 'they make time for you, which makes you feel better'; 'he's very approachable, you can relax with him'; and 'you don't feel hesitant, you can talk to her'. Above all, parents attach a great deal of importance to the way in which teachers demonstrate an awareness and sensitivity to their children's needs as well as care and concern about their progress. A shared concern for the child can play a significant part in the development of mutual respect between parent and teacher: one SENCO in this study elaborated on the relationship as follows:

> 'we've got to work closely together – there are some crucial issues to respond to – there are always differences of opinion, and we've got to have a mutual respect for one another, for each other's perception and point of view, and for where we're actually coming from in terms of the student'.
>
> (Beveridge, 1997: 65)

SENCOs have a particular role to fulfil concerning regular liaison with parents, and it is vital that they are committed to two-way communication. However, if home–school relationships are to be as beneficial as possible for children's learning, then such commitment must spread beyond SENCOs to the culture and ethos of the school as a whole. That is, there is a need for all staff to demonstrate their openness and willingness to listen, and a valuing of parental perspectives.

Involving parents in assessment, decision-making and review procedures

In their day-to-day family interactions, parents are in a prime position to observe, monitor and evaluate their children's development. Over the years, they build up an in-depth knowledge of their children which can, if accessed by school, add a great deal to teachers' understandings. In her review of the evidence from schemes that have sought to involve parents in the early assessment of their children in preschool and primary schools, Wolfendale (1992: 80) concludes that:

- parents have expertise in commenting on development;
- parents' intimate knowledge of their children can be described by them;
- parental information can complement professional information;
- the information can show up differing behaviour in different settings;
- the information can serve to highlight concerns regarding progress;
- parents can provide a realistic appraisal of their children.

This potential parental contribution is highlighted in the Code of Practice (DfES, 2001a), which makes it clear that parents should be fully involved at every stage in the school-based assessment of children with special educational needs. Indeed, the Code emphasises that parents may be the first to identify the difficulties that their children are experiencing, and therefore schools need to have in place procedures for responding to expressions of parental concern.

The participation of parents of children with special educational needs in statutory assessment procedures has a comparatively long history, having been introduced by the 1981 Education Act. Research into parental experiences of these formal procedures has offered lessons that are of relevance for teachers in developing their approach to working with parents in the ongoing school-based cycle of assessment, decision-making and review that is required by the Code of Practice. It is evident, for example, that formal assessment can be stressful for parents and, while they typically wish for a full investigation of their children's difficulties, they can at the same time feel ambivalent about the possible outcomes that may result from this. Further, they can also frequently feel distressed by the degree of emphasis that is placed on their child's weaknesses (P. Russell, 1991), and by the questions that they perceive are raised about their own parenting practices and skills (Galloway et al., 1994). Because of the complex and interactive nature of special educational needs, there is real scope for discrepancies in professional and parental views. Where this is so, Allan (1999) has argued that parental contributions are very often assigned lower status than those of professionals: that is, they are more likely to be described as 'opinions' or 'feelings', whereas professional judgements are seen as being objective and therefore more factually based. It is not unusual to hear a professional describe a parental assessment as 'unrealistic' and to view the parental perspective as contributing in some way to the difficulties their children are experiencing. Accordingly, when significant differences exist between parental and professional views, the professional judgement tends to dominate, and this can add greatly to family stress.

Such experiences of parental participation in statutory assessment indicate that, if schools are to work together successfully with parents in the ongoing assessment of their children's needs, then this requires a sensitivity to the personal and emotional investment that parenting involves. There can be few experiences less comfortable for parents than meetings with professionals that focus only on their children's difficulties, and there is an evident need to balance this with due attention to areas of comparative strength and strategies for building upon these. Similarly, parents will clearly find it stressful if they perceive that, in arriving at their judgements about the nature of their children's needs, staff are making unfounded assumptions about the learning context of home and the quality of support they provide for their children's education. They will also find it deeply unsatisfactory if they feel that their own views concerning their children's needs are not properly listened to or given due weight. Parents and teachers have distinctly different relationships with children and see them in contexts that make differing personal, social and cognitive demands of them. It is therefore to be expected that there will be discrepancies in parental and professional assessments of children's needs. Genuine respect for the in-depth knowledge and understanding that parents have concerning their own children must be based on an acknowledgement of what Dale (1996) has described as the 'legitimacy of dissent'. Rather than seeing differences between home and school views as necessarily problematic, therefore, what is required is a readiness on the part of schools to seek constructive strategies for reconciling different viewpoints. As the Code of Practice (DfES, 2001a) emphasises, both parents and teachers stand to gain an enhanced knowledge of children's needs if there is a two-way process of shared understandings and insights.

The involvement of parents in the review of their children's progress can take a number of forms, including parent–teacher consultations, written reporting and, for children with statements of special educational need, annual review procedures. Parents typically express a preference for individual meetings with their children's teachers above all other forms of communication with school, but this does not mean that such consultations are necessarily a positive experience for either parents or teachers. For example, both parties may come to the meeting with their own separate agendas which, if not acknowledged and explicitly addressed, can result in a frustrating occasion for all concerned. On the basis of his research, Bastiani (1992) has identified a number of factors associated with successful parent–teacher consultation meetings, in which both parties feel they have been able to contribute their perspectives. These include ensuring that parents have information about the precise nature, purpose and length of the meeting, and the opportunity to clarify and add to the agenda set by school; a constructive focus, which aims for agreed decisions about appropriate next steps to support and extend children's learning, and organisational arrangements that allow privacy and comfort. Even where these factors are borne in mind, though, some parents will require more reassurance and support than others in taking up the invitation to contribute to discussions about their children's educational progress. Their past relationships with school staff are likely to influence how readily they attend meetings: those whose previous contacts with teachers have been dominated by discussions of their children's problems are likely to feel at best apprehensive in their dealings with school, and others may feel diffident or lacking in confidence in what they can contribute to review meetings. In such cases, schools need to consider not only the range of opportunities that they provide for parents to become involved, but also the forms of assistance that may be needed in order to encourage parents to participate more fully.

Both parents and teachers tend to express a preference for informality, where possible, in consultation meetings. When their children have special educational needs, however, parents are also involved in more formal assessment and review procedures. It is apparent from research into their experiences that even those parents who feel confident in putting forward their views in informal meetings can feel like passive participants in these procedures, overwhelmed by the contributions of professionals. It is evident that professionals usually plan their own contributions to these meetings in considerable detail, and it is important that strategies be put in place by schools that will help parents feel equally well-prepared. Without this, parents may share the frustration expressed by one mother that 'unprepared, you're just on the defensive all the time' (Beveridge, 1997: 63). A number of researchers have presented structured frameworks that might be used to support parents in preparing their contributions (e.g. Wolfendale, 1988, 1993; Hughes and Carpenter, 1991; Hornby *et al.*, 1995), and some guidelines have also been provided in governmental publications (DfEE, 1997b; DfES 2001b). In the absence of some such structured support, it is rare for parents to feel that they have been able to contribute as active participants whose views have been given equal weight to those of the professionals involved.

It has long been recognised that, although parents have certain rights in relation to educational decision-making, the extent to which they exercise their rights will be limited unless they are sufficiently knowledgeable, informed and confident about their role (Wragg, 1989). Professional support of parental contributions therefore has a major part to play. However, Armstrong (1995) has pointed out that even those professionals who are committed to parental involvement can sometimes inadvertently raise barriers to their full participation. For example, they may be so familiar themselves with the formal assessment and review procedures that they misjudge parental understandings of these. Parents do not always appreciate the relevance or significance of the information that professionals provide, and this puts them at a marked disadvantage in any subsequent 'joint' decision-making. The feelings of powerlessness that parents can experience in this situation are not always recognised, because parents and professionals can come away from a meeting with very different perceptions of what has gone on. Thus, for example, whereas a professional may believe that the meeting has involved parents as full participants, parents may have seen its purpose as being to gain their agreement to a professional decision.

Further, it should be acknowledged that not all professionals are equally positive about the principle of parental involvement in educational decision-making, and that some hold ambivalent views. Mordaunt (2001), for example, has reported that some professionals argue that a perspective that is rooted in wanting the best for their children can 'cloud the judgement' of parents, particularly when their children have special educational needs. Others seek to draw a distinction between the sorts of decisions on which they believe parents have relevant expertise, such as their children's care and welfare, and other more purely educational concerns. There is little doubt that few parents feel fully confident in their knowledge of the formal academic curriculum, and most may well expect teachers to take the lead in decisions about appropriate interventions for their children. Nevertheless, the Code of Practice (DfES, 2001a) is explicit that schools should seek to take full account of parental perspectives when determining appropriate educational interventions for their children. Parents have their own priorities for their children, as well as insights concerning the sorts of strategies that might best meet their needs, and it can be argued that decision-making in school is more likely to be effective when teachers acknowledge and incorporate parental views. The importance of home–school collaboration in deciding on educational goals and how best to achieve these becomes heightened in situations where teachers ask parents to support school interventions by engaging in specific tasks with their child at home.

Involving parents in teaching their own children

As discussed in Chapter 3, parents play a key role in facilitating their children's learning through their shared activities and daily routines at home. Many schools, particularly though not exclusively during the primary years, seek to capitalise on the powerful educational resource that parents represent by involving them in more formal teaching activities with their children at home (Jowett *et al.*, 1991). Some initiatives are focused on children with special educational needs, especially during the secondary school years, but in the earlier years an underlying principle is that many potential areas of difficulty might be prevented if parents can be fully involved.

Much of the evidence for the effectiveness of active parental involvement in school-directed learning comes from research into the teaching of reading. In her seminal research in this field, Hewison and her colleagues observed that children's levels of reading attainment were strongly associated with whether their mothers regularly listened to them reading at home (Hewison and Tizard, 1980). On the basis of this finding, they went on to implement a major intervention study, designed to establish whether parental help with reading would demonstrably lead to enhanced reading performance. They were able to show that, over a two-year period, children in a parental involvement group made significant gains in their reading by comparison with others (Tizard *et al.*, 1982). Furthermore, the teachers and parents involved in the study reported wider benefits too: the children showed generally enhanced progress with their schoolwork, and home–school relationships were said to have been improved through the experience of collaboration. These results were sufficiently robust to show a lasting impact when the children were followed up subsequently on transfer to secondary school (Hewison, 1988).

Reading has a central place in formal education and many of the special educational needs that children experience at school are associated with difficulties in reading. It is not surprising therefore that children's progress in learning to read is typically seen as a priority by both parents and teachers. Hewison's research provided an impetus for the development of a number of other schemes that sought to involve parents in their children's reading. The breadth and variety of approaches that have been adopted have been reviewed in Topping and Wolfendale (1985) and, while not all have been equally rigorously evaluated, most report gains both in children's reading skills as well as in more general aspects of their learning and behaviour at school. Initiatives have subsequently been introduced for preschool children (e.g. Hannon, 1995), and others have broadened the focus to encompass family literacy (Wolfendale and Topping, 1995). The success of parental involvement in reading has also spurred developments in further areas of the curriculum, such as mathematics (e.g. Merttens and Vass, 1993; Fraser and Honeyford, 2000) and science (e.g. Topping, 1998).

While there is a great deal of evidence for the effectiveness of well-planned schemes of parental involvement, Gregory (2000) has raised questions concerning the assumptions that underpin most approaches. Projects that seek to involve parents in the teaching of reading typically ask parents to work with their children in particular ways using specific school-directed materials, but Gregory's argument is that it is inappropriate to assume that the same approach is suitable for all families. She puts forward three inter-related principles for developing strategies that are more responsive to diverse linguistic and cultural family backgrounds. First, she points out the need to go beyond a narrow reliance on story books and to acknowledge that there are different sorts of literacy experiences and knowledge that children gain at home and in their community activities. Second, she highlights the importance of extending the focus to incorporate participation not only by parents but by other family members and also, where appropriate, by other significant individuals and settings beyond the family, such as community classes and clubs. Finally, she argues that the aim of family involvement schemes should not be to replicate the school's approach to learning at home, but rather to find ways of building bridges between the learning of home and school. The questions that Gregory raises and the principles that she puts forward with respect to home–school collaboration in literacy have equal applicability to other areas of the curriculum, and they serve as a valuable reminder of the need for schools to develop their approaches in ways that both acknowledge and respond to significant aspects of family diversity.

At the level of the individual family, diversity is associated with the dynamics of roles, relationships and routines which exist between and among all its members. Parents hold varied beliefs both about what it is that constitutes teaching and also about the extent to which it is an integral part of their parental role, as discussed in Chapter 3. Depending on the nature and range of the competing demands on their attention, time and energy, parents also vary in the priority which they are able to afford to active collaboration with school. Further, although there is evidence that parents generally wish to know whether there are things that they can do to support their children's learning at home (Coleman, 1998), this does not necessarily imply that 'school-like' activities are readily compatible with their natural parenting approach. The parent–child relationship is usually characterised by an intense emotional intimacy that is quite different from the nature of a teacher–pupil relationship and, while many parents engage successfully in explicit teaching activities with their children, others find it a stressful experience. When this is so, it can be counterproductive to their relationship for parents and children to work on school tasks together directly, and attention needs to be given to other ways in which home learning experiences can complement those of school.

A recognition of the significance of issues associated with family diversity becomes even more important when children have special educational needs, because of the strong emphasis that is typically placed on active home–school collaboration. Parents of children with developmental delays and impairments are encouraged by professionals to see teaching and, in many cases, therapy as a significant part of their role, and research suggests that most appear to do so (Mittler and Mittler, 1982). However, there is also evidence that they can feel anxious about the extent of the responsibility that is placed on them to carry out special programmes at home, and guilty that they should be doing more (Dale, 1996; Beveridge, 1997). Like other parents, they are less likely to feel pressured in this way if they fully participate with school staff in discussions and decision-making concerning the nature of any intervention that is to be carried out; which family members, friends and others might be directly involved; and how it can be implemented in ways that take account of the family routines and activities that go to make up the learning context of home.

Involving parents in behaviour management

Parents are powerful role models and sources of reinforcement for their children, and there is a long history of clinical work involving parents in behaviour management programmes when their children show behavioural difficulties (e.g. Elliott and Place, 1998). In contrast, there have been comparatively few systematic and documented schemes for home–school collaboration in this area of work. This is somewhat surprising, given that there is a recognition in national policy that parents and teachers need to cooperate together in this area. For example, the Elton Report on discipline in schools (DES, 1989) emphasised the importance of parental participation in the development of school policy, and a key aspect of the home–school agreements that were introduced by legislation in 1998 concerns discipline and behaviour. Miller (2003) has reviewed the available evidence on the effectiveness of parental involvement schemes that focus on behaviour management issues. The most common form is one that capitalises on the access that parents have to a wider range of sanctions and privileges than are available for teachers: parents are typically asked to apply these at home in response to regular reports on their child's behaviour at school. Although Miller cites evidence that well-planned and systematic home reporting strategies of this kind can be successful in improving children's behaviour at home, there is clearly the potential for more genuinely collaborative work in this area.

However, a number of sensitive issues arise if schools are to work together with parents on the management of their children's behaviour in this way. For example, although both parents and teachers are typically concerned about problematic behaviour, they may hold differing values and beliefs, which lead to different perspectives about what constitutes appropriate or inappropriate behaviour, and about the influences that contribute to this. Further, as children can and do behave differently in different contexts, it can be the case that parents and teachers do not see the same range of behaviours, and as a result they each may have a differing focus for their concerns. It should be noted, too, that parents often have little knowledge or familiarity with particular aspects of school life, and as a result will not always be in a good position to understand why their child is misbehaving at school. Behaviour that they perceive as difficult challenges both parents and teachers, and can have an adverse effect on their sense of their own competence. In such situations, it is tempting to look for oversimplified causes of the problem rather than to acknowledge the complex interacting factors that are likely to be involved. The emotional impact on parents when their children experience significant and lasting difficulties can be intense, incorporating feelings of anxiety, uncertainty, shame and guilt. These emotions are likely to be compounded when, as frequently happens, they feel that they are held responsible and blamed for their children's misbehaviour in school (Sambrook and Gray, 2002). Such feelings are likely to lead to parental defensiveness: as teachers may themselves feel undermined and lacking in confidence as a result of particular classroom behaviours, and may also become defensive as a result, this creates real obstacles for successful home–school communication. For this reason it has been argued that a key aim of schools when seeking parental involvement in relation to problematic behaviour must be 'to try to reduce the blame and stigma associated with emotional and behavioural difficulties and to "set the scene" for more positive and collaborative working' (Sambrook and Gray, 2002: 46).

Effective strategies for involving parents must be underpinned by a whole-school approach, in which due recognition is given to the influence not only of home, but also of school and the home–school relationship, in contributing to children's behaviour. Wolfendale (1986), for example, proposes a model which begins with an appraisal of a school's curricular and pastoral provision and their influence upon pupil behaviour. She advocates a preventative approach to collaboration, both by involving parents in the development of school policy and procedures for promoting good behaviour, and also by developing active cooperation on positive aspects of their children's learning. She argues that this is a necessary starting point in order to ensure that, when the need arises for direct home–school interventions focused on specific problems, this is built upon a positive foundation. The way in which Wolfendale's model might be implemented is illustrated in the account by Morgan and Piccos (1997) of how one primary school went about developing its strategy. The main elements of the whole school approach that was adopted are summarised in Box 5.1. This highlights the importance given to ensuring a consistency of approach

---

Box 5.1 Illustration of a whole-school approach to parental involvement in behaviour management

- In-service training on behaviour management for whole-school staff
- Consultation with parents on school behaviour policy
- Review of curricular arrangements for children showing problematic behaviour
- Provision of lunch-time and after-school clubs
- Review of procedures for internal school communication and incident reporting
- Strengthening of parental involvement strategy
- Provision of better-quality information about school for parents
- For particular children, regular parental contact to design, implement and review individual behaviour contracts
- Establishment of a parent support group.

(adapted from Morgan and Piccos, 1997)

across all school staff, through the provision of in-service training and the development of effective within-school channels for
communication. Attention was also given to the impact of curricular arrangements on groups of pupils and to the potential support
that could be offered through lunch-time and after-school clubs.

All aspects of the school's parental involvement procedures were
reviewed and strengthened, not only those directly associated with
problematic behaviour. However, specific home–school interventions for children whose behaviour caused particular concern
were introduced in the form of individual contracts. In response to
a number of parents who requested guidance on common behaviour
management issues that they were facing at home, such as non-
compliance, bedtime routines, sibling rivalry and so on, the school
also set up a parent support group. It is perhaps important to
note that one of the main outcomes arising from participation in
this group was reported to be an improvement in home–school
communication.

It has been emphasised throughout this discussion that, if individual home–school collaborations are to be developed with respect
to behaviour management, then ideally these need to be set against
the context of a whole-school approach in which systematic strategies have been put in place to establish positive parent–teacher
relationships and mutual trust. Where this is so, the evidence from
clinical research is that parents are likely to be willing and moti-
vated participants, provided that they see the problem as a significant one that is within their capacity to deal with. In order to
generate the conditions that will support this, schools need to allow
time for parents and staff to share perspectives and come to an
agreed view on what appears to be the nature of the behaviour
management problem, what the contributing factors may be and
what intervention strategies might be effective. This requires an
alertness to different aspects of family diversity, for example in
roles, relationships and routines, which were referred to earlier in
the context of schemes to involve parents in teaching activities
with their children. It is evident too that, if parents experience
stress at home as a result of their children's difficult behaviour,
this can limit the reserves that they are able to draw on in order to
focus on specific behaviour management strategies. Related to this,
it is particularly important to acknowledge that some of the techniques that might be used by teachers are neither manageable
within the home situation nor possible to use within the context of

an emotionally close parent–child relationship. Rather than seeking for identical parent and teacher strategies, therefore, the aim should be for compatibility between approaches at home and at school. Even when working on jointly agreed strategies, it is not unusual for teachers as well as parents to feel anxiety and the need for reassurance about the degree of success with which they tackle behaviour management issues. There is a need therefore to make continuing time available to allow for the sort of shared monitoring of progress that will allow mutual support and confidence-building to take place. It is important to note too that relevant support services may have a key role to play in the development of this work: indeed, their involvement can become crucial if there is a breakdown of trust and communication between home and school to be overcome (Dowling and Pound, 1994; Sambrook and Gray, 2002; Miller, 2003).

Building positive relationships

If the potential benefits of home–school collaboration are to be realised, then this requires explicit whole-school strategies designed to promote constructive parent–teacher relationships. It is fundamental to the establishment of such strategies that schools support all of their staff in developing the positive attitudes, commitment, sensitivity and skill that are necessary for successful interactions with parents. There are clearly practical constraints for schools in the extent to which they can be responsive to the full range of individual diversity among parents and families. Nevertheless, it is essential that procedures for communicating with and involving parents be sufficiently flexible to take account of variation in family circumstances. At the very least, consideration needs to be given to ways of eliciting and responding to family priorities and preferences, and ways of providing appropriate help where needed in order to support parental participation in educational processes. Further, if schools wish parents to take part in joint activities with staff as co-teachers or managers of their children's behaviour, then steps must be taken to ensure that what they are asking is manageable in the home context and will not inadvertently contribute to family stress. These considerations become particularly significant in the case of children with special educational needs, when it can be argued that sensitivity to the parental and family perspective is even more essential. A responsiveness to family diversity also implies the acknowledgement that parents will vary in their ability, availability and willingness to take up specific opportunities for involvement in their children's schooling. Rather than make assumptions, for example about a potential lack of interest on the part of particular families, however, the challenge for schools is to seek ways of reaching out to those parents who appear to be most diffident about what it is they have to contribute to their children's formal education.

The nature and extent of parental involvement not only vary from family to family, but also vary for the same family at different phases of their children's schooling. It is not unusual, for example, for parents to feel that, as their children begin to grow in independence and in identification with their peer group, so they should take a less actively intervening role in relation to school. This shift is typically associated with the transition from primary to secondary school. What appears to be most significant from the perspective of their children, is not necessarily the number or range of contacts between their parents and teachers so much as the quality of the relationship that is built up over time. The greater the level of mutual trust, understanding and respect between home and school, the more confident children are likely to feel about the support they have for their educational progress. The promotion of children's well-being, progress and achievements at school represents the central purpose of parent–teacher communication and, unquestionably, this is a purpose in which the children themselves must be seen to play an active role. Their participation in parent–teacher communication and the developing home–school relationship forms the focus of the next chapter.

Chapter 6

Children's participation in the home–school relationship

It has been emphasised in the previous chapter that children are the focus of home–school communication, and that their well-being and progress must form the central purpose when seeking to promote constructive teacher–parent relationships. Children are not only the focus, but can also exert a strong influence on the nature of the relationships that are established. Where children get on well with their teachers and feel valued and included by them as important members of their learning community, their parents are likely to be well-disposed towards collaboration with school. In contrast, where teacher–child relationships are negative, this can create a major barrier to successful home–school communication. Despite the central role that children play, however, schools do not always plan for their active participation in home–school communication in an explicit and systematic way. This is surprising, given the increased attention that has been paid in recent years to the need to listen to children's perspectives on issues that concern them. The case for active participation by pupils in educational processes has been outlined in earlier chapters. Rooted in the recognition that children are not simply passive recipients of learning processes, but are social agents in their own right, there has been a growing acknowledgement that children have a personal perspective on their own experiences, aspirations and needs which cannot be inferred from having adults speak on their behalf (Beresford, 1997). Accordingly it has gradually become more widely accepted that children have the right to have a voice in decisions that affect them. In the context of their formal education, 'having a voice' can relate both to whole-school policies and practices and also to their individual learning experiences.

At a school-wide level, there is evidence that where staff demonstrate a respect for pupils' views and involve them in decision-making, this can serve to enhance self-esteem (Jelly *et al.*, 2000), promote positive relationships (Alderson, 2000) and help to prevent disaffection (Cox, 2000). Such findings have clear implications for children with special educational needs, not least because unless there are explicit strategies in place to support it, those who struggle most in their learning are least likely to have their voices heard. For this reason, it is pertinent to note that pupil participation has been identified as a key component of combating educational disadvantage and developing successful inclusive practice (e.g. Cox, 2000; Thomas *et al.*, 1998).

At an individual level, children's motivation and confidence are certainly likely to be enhanced when they are encouraged to feel in control of their own learning. Wolfendale (1987), for example, has proposed that teachers have a responsibility to help all children to:

- understand the point and purpose of the learning tasks presented to them and in which they engage;
- learn how to learn;
- evolve effective learning strategies;
- identify learning hurdles, 'sticking points' along the way, and apply appropriate problem-solving learning strategies.

(Wolfendale, 1987: 37)

Wolfendale's argument offers a clear illustration of the ways in which children's active participation in the process of target-setting and reflection upon their own educational achievements and needs can act to support the learning process. It follows, therefore, that there are strong educational grounds for involving children in explicit discussion of their learning and progress. From this perspective, the sorts of parent–teacher communication that were discussed in the previous chapter can all be seen to have the potential for direct involvement of children. Indeed, where children have special educational needs, it is a requirement of the Code of Practice (DfES, 2001a) that both they and their parents must be involved in ongoing assessment, decision-making and review processes.

Children's views and those of their parents and teachers do not necessarily correspond, of course, and a number of writers have drawn attention to the tensions that exist between the principles of parental partnership and pupil participation (e.g. Brannen *et al.*,

2000; Wyness, 2000). In particular, they highlight the risk that a focus on parental rights can predominate to such an extent that children's rights are overlooked. However, it need not necessarily be the case that the involvement of parents inhibits that of their children. Children need support from both their parents and their teachers if they are to participate fully in educational processes. The challenge therefore is to find ways in which home–school communication can serve to facilitate rather than restrict the role of children as active participants in decision-making and review. In order to explore what may be involved in this process, the following discussion briefly considers the nature of children's participation in decision-making both at home and at school and highlights the potential that exists for parents and teachers to gain mutual support from each other with respect to this area of children's learning. It then focuses on the scope for enhancing children's participation through systematically planned involvement in the context of home–school communication.

Children's participation at home

Bronfenbrenner (1979) has described the ways in which learning at home is facilitated by interactions that become progressively more complex and demanding over time, and where the developing child gradually gains increased self-direction. Children's learning experiences within the family context are frequently initiated by them, and therefore are typically focused on and shaped by their own interests. Further, as discussed in Chapter 3, children are not only active participants in their own learning, but they also contribute in important ways to whole-family life. As the mature members of the family, parents and other adult relatives clearly have both a powerful influence and significant responsibilities in relation to their children's welfare. Nevertheless it is equally evident that children themselves can and do fulfil a substantial role in providing both practical and emotional support within their families (e.g. Brannen *et al.*, 2000). Thus, through reciprocal activities and mutual support, there builds up over time an interdependence between family members in which children, as well as adults, play a key part.

   The nature of learning experiences at home and the extent of the interdependence that develops between family members has led a number of researchers to draw attention to the greater range of opportunities that exist for children to exercise autonomy and participate in decision-making at home by comparison with school (e.g. Mayall, 2001). Box 6.1 exemplifies just some of the decision-making opportunities that children can experience at home. As illustrated, these opportunities may be focused primarily on children's own activities and routines; they may involve more complex negotiations with another family member such as a brother or sister in order to arrive at shared decisions; or, in some cases, they may require participation in discussions in which the wishes and preferences of all family members need to be taken into account and any necessary compromises reached.

Although there is potentially more scope for children to be involved as active participants in decision-making at home than at school, parents clearly vary in the extent to which they encourage this. They are influenced in their approach by their views concerning age-appropriate expectations for children in general, as well as by their assessment of their own children's competence and maturity. It is evident that these judgements can also be affected by gender and cultural variables (Brannen, 1996; Morrow, 1998). It should be noted too that, even among parents who endorse the idea that their children have the right to participate in family decision-making, there can be difficulties and uncertainties in putting this principle into practice. For example, it is apparent that it is not a simple matter to achieve a balance between the needs and rights of all family members. Further, there are complexities involved in

---

Box 6.1 Children's decision-making at home

Own activities and routines	e.g. choosing clothes visits with friends homework holiday bedtimes etc.
Shared activities and routines, with sibling or other family member	e.g. choosing meals access to TV or video use of bedroom space etc.
Whole-family activities and routines	e.g. household rules family outings holiday etc.

trying to reconcile parental responsibilities related to care, protection and discipline with the wish to promote their children's independence.

Such dilemmas come to the fore in relation to the personal safety of children outside of the home and family context. They are heightened too when children have special needs, for the more vulnerable that parents see their children to be, the greater the anxiety they are likely to feel about the level of independence that is possible for them. In cases where children have limited communication skills, additional complexities also arise. The nature of their choices and preferences can be difficult to establish and parents typically find that they have to interpret and make decisions on their children's behalf. This mediation role is often a very important one for parents of children with special educational needs, but at the same time, there can be difficulties in moving beyond advocacy to the support of their children's active participation in decision-making. For example, parents can find that strategies that encourage their children to express their own views and preferences do not 'come naturally' and further, that it is difficult to adopt a consistent approach with clear distinctions between what is and is not negotiable.

In broad terms, the home context can be characterised as one in which there is a wide range of opportunities for children to express choices and preferences and negotiate decisions with other family members. As a result, although their approach and expectations vary, parents typically have extensive knowledge and experience of their children's participation in decision-making at home. However, because they may also experience difficulties and uncertainties concerning the promotion of their children's autonomy, they can feel the need for reassurance in this area, for example from other parents, friends and relatives or from their children's schools. This need is likely to be particularly significant when their children have severe or complex needs.

Children's participation at school

By comparison with the potential of their home and family situations, the curriculum, timetabling and procedural routines of school life constrain the opportunities for children to be actively participant in decision-making. Nevertheless, a number of approaches

Box 6.2 Decision-making at school

Curriculum	e.g. individual learning targets personal, social and health education circle time citizenship education
Pastoral arrangements	e.g. peer support systems peer mediation class rules
School policy	e.g. School Council.

have been developed within schools that offer some degree of involvement for their pupils, as illustrated in Box 6.2. At an individual level, involvement in the setting of learning targets is an increasingly established practice and, as part of the formal personal, social and health education curriculum, children may be explicitly helped to monitor their own progress. Through activities such as circle time, they are involved in whole-class discussions aimed at encouraging the cooperative and open sharing of views with their teachers and peers, and citizenship education classes can serve to facilitate increased understanding of their own rights and responsibilities as well as those of others. Pastoral arrangements too can support pupil participation, for example in peer mediation systems or through full group involvement in the establishing of class rules.

The extent of the involvement that children perceive they actually have in such activities is dependent on a school ethos that explicitly emphasises listening to pupils and treating their views as of value. This requires the sort of commitment and consistency of approach across all staff that is not necessarily easy to achieve. Pupils often comment on the inconsistency of their experiences at school, and it is not unusual to find them expressing the view that they are neither listened to by staff nor trusted to make decisions (Alderson, 2002). For these reasons, some argue that there is a need for a formal means of ensuring that children have a voice in relation to the development of school policy, for example by the establishment of a School Council of elected pupil representatives. The provision of an effective School Council has been described by Alderson (2000) on the basis of her research as 'a key practical and symbolic indicator of respect for children's rights' (p. 124), and it is certainly the case that children who have experience of this tend to endorse the view that it is a valuable means of putting across their perspective to staff.

For whole-school commitment and consistency of practice to be developed, there is also an evident need for clarity in communication about the nature and extent of pupil involvement that is possible or desirable in differing situations. Without this, it is not unusual to find divergent teacher and pupil perspectives concerning the level of participation that takes place. Taking just one example from Box 6.2 as an illustration, staff frequently describe procedures whereby they discuss and agree a set of class rules together with their pupils at the beginning of the school year. How this is done, and the degree of genuine pupil participation that is involved, are clearly likely to differ for different teachers and with different age groups. However, the children concerned are typically well aware that the teacher will play the major part in determining what rules are adopted, and therefore the purpose of the discussions may not be experienced by them as shared decision-making at all. For instance, the process was described as follows by one group of primary pupils: 'we put up our hands to make suggestions. If (the teacher) likes it she'll put it up (on the board), if not she'll leave it out' (Beveridge, 2004). This example, which is far from unique, serves to illustrate why an explicit vocabulary for describing pupil participation must be seen as a minimum requirement for the building of a whole-school approach and a shared understanding between children and their teachers.

The need for clarity becomes even more apparent with respect to home–school liaison. It has been argued earlier in this chapter that children need the support of both their parents and their teachers if they are to build the required skills and confidence to participate as fully as possible in educational processes, and therefore it is important that this be explicitly addressed within the context of parent–teacher communication. Sensitivity on the part of both parents and teachers is required in order to ensure that children are neither underestimated concerning their competence to be involved, nor pressured by excessive demands. Potentially parents and teachers have mutual support to offer each other in this task: that is, the wider knowledge and experience that parents have concerning their children's decision-making can be drawn upon to inform and extend school practice; and at the same time, those parents who seek it may derive reassurance from discussion with school staff about the approach they take at home to their children's developing autonomy.

Children's participation and parent–teacher communication

Some researchers (e.g. Edwards, 2002) have criticised current approaches to home–school collaboration as being too focused on parents and teachers, and argue that this distracts attention from the voice of the child in educational decision-making. However, it need not necessarily be the case that a working relationship between their parents and teachers has an adverse impact on children's developing autonomy, as a study by Ericsson and Larsen (2002) has demonstrated. These two Norwegian researchers set out to explore the evidence concerning contrasting effects that might potentially arise from close home–school liaison: they speculated that, on the one hand, it could lead parents and teachers to join forces in a way that increases the amount of adult control that children experience; conversely, however, it could provide a context within which children are able to use adult support in order to gain greater participation in decision-making both at home and at school. From their observations of 7- and 13-year-old children taking part in parent–teacher meetings, they found that there were clear instances of the former effect. For example, they portrayed some parents and teachers as adopting the type of joint approach which, while 'benevolent and well-meaning', restricted the children's role to one of endorsing the adults' perspectives and decisions. Further, in extreme cases, they reported children as 'fighting for autonomy' by trying to prevent their parents from becoming too closely involved in school matters. By contrast, though, they also reported situations in which children were 'recognised participants in their own education, entitled to an opinion, and empowered by the parents' presence' (Ericsson and Larsen, 2002: 98). Thus, for example, they observed shy children using their parents to speak up for them at meetings, and others who appeared to derive the necessary confidence from their parents' company which enabled them to articulate their views for themselves and to effect changes at school as a result.

Parent–teacher consultations are typically a central component of home–school liaison, and there is evident potential to use them as a vehicle for involving children in educational decision-making. However, this potential is not always acknowledged and children are not always encouraged to attend. In the UK, different schools have differing policies and a frequently heard concern among staff, particularly with respect to younger pupils, is that children's presence can act to inhibit full and frank discussion between parents and teachers. Parents may also hold varied views about the desirability or otherwise of including children in meetings: some consider that it will add to a fuller understanding between all concerned about the nature of their educational progress and needs, and others express a concern that it might be an overwhelming experience and a source of anxiety for their children. Children's own perspectives may be more robust, however, even when they recognise that parents and teachers are not always completely open in their presence. Not all find attendance at consultation meetings easy, of course, and they may report feelings of nervousness (e.g. Crozier, 2000). However, despite this they frequently assert that they want to be present in order to hear both their parents' and their teachers' views. In one study of teacher, parent and pupil perceptions, for example, most children at both primary and secondary school expressed the strong belief that they should be included in parent–teacher consultations, in order to be properly informed of both positive and negative things that were being said about their educational progress (Beveridge, 2004). A sample of their comments gives the flavour of the views that were typically expressed:

> 'It's you they're talking about' (boy, aged 10 years);
> 'It's not the same when your mum tells you – you should get the whole information from the teacher' (girl, aged 9 years);
> 'Mum doesn't tell me all the details – she only tells you the things that are good and there could have been things that were bad, but she doesn't tell me any of that' (girl, aged 9 years);
> 'You get more from it, you feel more involved' (girl, aged 13 years).

Further, in common with Ericsson and Larsen's (2002) findings, there was some evidence in this study that the presence of their parents in meetings could also be experienced as empowering. Thus, a number of children explained that they could have a different style of interaction with teachers when their parents were present: for example, they found that they were able to ask questions and disagree with their judgements in a way that was not possible to do in the classroom context.

Parent–teacher consultations are sometimes directly linked to formal written material, such as annual reports on children's progress and attainments. These sorts of written reports clearly have the potential to act as a starting point for constructive two- and three-way discussions between parents, teachers and children, where schools choose to use them in this way. The positive response that children may bring to explicit and systematic involvement of this kind can be illustrated by the views expressed by one primary school pupil when he said: 'I think it's good when we get these letters home. I think teachers should be more like my mum. Because every year when we get a letter home about how I've done we sit down and we go through it – I think that's what the teachers should do' (boy, aged 10, in Beveridge, 2004). However, although it is evident that it is possible to use such focused discussions as a means of promoting participation, it is important to acknowledge that children's physical presence in meetings does not automatically lead to their genuine inclusion as active participants. Rather, as Ericsson and Larsen's (2002) study demonstrates, positive participation requires skill and understanding on the part of the adults concerned and the development of strategies that demonstrate a responsiveness to and valuing of the children's perspectives.

Nowhere is this requirement more apparent than in the situation where children have special educational needs. Although the Code of Practice (DfES, 2001a) makes it clear that they should be as fully participant as possible in all aspects of educational decision-making, it is not unusual to find that their competence to be involved is underestimated (e.g. Rose, 1998; Wyness, 2000). As a result, they may face real barriers both in making their perspectives known and in having them taken seriously. Section 4 of the SEN Toolkit which accompanies the Code of Practice (DfES, 2001b) emphasises the importance of promoting children's participation in the development of their IEPs as follows:

> Wherever possible pupils should be involved in setting their own targets for the IEP, in agreeing and implementing appropriate strategies, and evaluating the outcomes.
>
> (DfES, 2001b, Section 4, para 21)

This principle is in line with evidence that children with special educational needs achieve more when they are included in the negotiation of targets and the identification of barriers to their learning (e.g. de Pear, 1997), and that IEPs can play a more significant part in their learning experiences when they feel they have ownership of them (e.g. Hart, 1998; Pearson, 2000). However, the challenges that are involved in its implementation should be acknowledged. With any child, teachers can find difficulties in moving beyond ensuring a familiarity with individual learning targets to developing an informed understanding of the basis for their selection. Similarly, although it is relatively straightforward to explain procedural aspects of the monitoring process, it can be a far more complex task to communicate the nature of the judgements that are involved when assessing progress. These difficulties are clearly likely to be compounded where children's special needs involve cognitive and communicative limitations, and there can be an understandable temptation on the part of both parents and teachers to speak for children rather than to elicit their own views directly. The Code of Practice (DfES, 2001a) is alert to the risk that parents can get into the habit of 'talking for' their children, and draws attention to the skills that teachers need if they are to ensure that both parental and child perspectives are heard and given due weight. It pays less attention, however, to the mutual safeguards and support that might potentially operate between parents and teachers where both are committed to helping children develop the necessary confidence and skills for genuine participation.

There is no doubt that children are more likely to become fully participant in educational processes when there is sustained and well-planned collaboration between their parents and teachers that is designed to support this. It can be expected, for example, that the sorts of strategies that have been described by Jelly et al. (2000) for the progressive involvement of children with learning difficulties in target-setting and the development of their IEPs will be more effective where parents and teachers work on these together. Experience of supported involvement in these less formal sorts of activities appears to be a fundamental requirement if children are also to take part in more formal contexts. Where children have statements of special educational need, for example, they should have the opportunity to contribute to annual review meetings, along with their parents, teachers and other involved professionals. In practice, not all children choose to attend these reviews and, depending on the nature of their needs, they might gain little from doing so. Whether physically present or not, however, they are likely not only to be more capable of contributing their views but also to have greater confidence that their perspective will be respected and valued, if they have built up positive experiences of participation in less formal decision-making contexts. It might be added too that parents and teachers themselves are likely to gain from such practice, which should enable them gradually to build up familiarity and ease as well as the necessary skills for an open negotiation of decisions which take account of both their own views and those of the children concerned. The need for all parties to become as practised and skilled in joint decision-making as possible becomes particularly apparent during transition planning for post-school options, where the evidence to date suggests that the formality of the Code of Practice procedures (DfES, 2001a) does not support young people's participation, and that adult views tend to dominate (e.g. Broomhead, 1998; Dee, 2002).

The particular demands of formal review and transition procedures serve to highlight the importance of planning for continuity and progression in the development of children's participation experiences, and this applies for all children, not only those with special educational needs. Within the context of the home–school relationship, such planning clearly needs to be informed by the evolving nature of parental involvement as children progress through their school careers. In line with their recognition of their children's growing autonomy, parents typically become less directly involved in their education as they move from primary into secondary school. However, it should not be assumed that children at secondary school necessarily wish for a reduction in the level of their parents' involvement. Children of all ages frequently continue to see their parents as important advocates on their behalf, and as such they ascribe them a significant role not only throughout school but also in post-school choices and decisions. Morrow (1998), for example, has described how children of early secondary school age express a wish to be consulted and listened to, but at the same time perceive a need for adult support and do not want to be given full responsibility for decisions that affect their lives. Her findings are also reflected in Crozier's (2000) study of children's views of parental support during their secondary school years. Both younger and older pupils reported that they wanted their parents to be involved in their schooling, but the oldest expected to have a greater degree of control over the form of the involvement and described ways in which they actively sought to manage this. Studies such as these have clear implications for schools, for they indicate that increasing participation in educational decision-making by children as they grow older does not necessarily imply a decreased level of participation by their parents, but rather the negotiation of a different form of involvement.

Extending the home–school relationship

Home-school relationships have long been recognised as significant in promoting children's educational achievements. It has been argued in this chapter that there is scope for extending the home–school relationship in ways that are explicitly aimed at enhancing children's participation in decision-making processes. Currently, there is considerable variation in school practice with respect to the inclusion of children in parent–teacher communication. Adapting Treseder's (1997) continuum, this ranges from instances where children are *aware* of communications that are taking place, through situations in which they are *informed* and *consulted*, to a greater degree of *active participation*. This variation not only reflects the age and ability of the children concerned, but also a school's policy and commitment to their involvement.

The implementation of the Code of Practice (DfES, 2001a) requires schools to review and make more systematic their procedures for ensuring the participation of both parents and children in educational decision-making. While this may be seen as of particular significance for children with special educational needs, it necessitates the sort of whole-school approach that can only be of benefit for all children and parents. Clearly there are individual differences between children in the extent to which they wish to take part directly in formal procedures of consultation and review, and similarly there will be variation among parents and teachers in how comfortable they feel about speaking freely when children are present. However, confidence and participation skills can be built up through less formal means, provided that certain conditions are met. These conditions include clarity in communication about the purpose, nature and extent of the participation that is aimed for, coupled with a shared understanding and commitment by parents and teachers to provide children with the support that they may need.

Alldred *et al.* (2002) have pointed out that a common motivation in the development of parental involvement policies has been to break down the barriers between home and school. If the home–school relationship is to be extended in the way argued in this chapter, it is important to acknowledge that there are aspects of their home lives that children will wish to keep private. Accordingly there is an evident need for sensitivity to the ways in which they may seek to 'manage the gap' between home and school on their own terms. Nevertheless, it is also apparent that children typically see their parents as potential mediators on their behalf with school and, as demonstrated throughout the preceding discussion, that there is real scope for developing home–school communication in ways that give priority to the promotion of their involvement as key participants.

Chapter 7

Towards partnership and participation

This chapter focuses on the ideas that underpin the notion of home–school partnership, drawing attention to those qualities in the interaction that might distinguish partnerships from other forms of cooperation. There are considerable complexities surrounding parent–teacher relationships which need to be acknowledged, and which add to the challenges posed for staff. Despite the difficulties that arise, however, it can be argued that there is a need not only to aim for a working partnership with parents, but also to extend the relationship to include the participation of other involved professionals and, most importantly, the children themselves. The principles of participation and partnership are fundamental to much current educational thinking and the chapter concludes with some brief reflections on their place within the context of inclusive school practice.

The significance of home–school relationships

It has been a central theme of this book that home–school relationships have an essential role to play in promoting children's educational progress. Bronfenbrenner's ecological model (1977) demonstrates that children's needs at school cannot be seen in isolation from their learning in other settings, the first and most significant of which is their home and family. Parents are typically not only the primary caregivers but also the first educators of their children and, from their earliest interactions onwards, they are intimately involved in supporting all aspects of their development. The children themselves are active contributors to this process: the varied roles that they develop both with their parents and with other family members and the mutual interdependencies that are established over time, all serve to reinforce the strong and enduring influence of the learning context that home represents. However, Bronfenbrenner's framework not only reflects the fundamental role of the family in children's development, but also provides a theoretical explanation for the importance of home–school relationships. That is, it proposes that the success with which children make the transition from home-based learning to the more formal expectations of school will be significantly affected by the quality of the communication between the two settings. From this perspective, the greater the gap that children experience between the learning demands of home and school, the greater the need for schools to give particular consideration to the ways in which they can promote good home–school links.

Over time, a great deal of empirical evidence has accumulated that supports Bronfenbrenner's position concerning the significance of the home–school relationship. Reference has been made in previous chapters to some of this evidence: for example, early intervention programmes have been found to be most effective where parents have been fully involved; children have been found to make significant gains in reading and show enhanced motivation for school-based learning when their parents and teachers have collaborated together; and overall school effectiveness has been associated with positive parental and community relationships. This sort of evidence has led to a growing acknowledgement, therefore, that educational professionals will generally be more effective in their roles and interventions where they develop cooperative relationships with children's parents.

In parallel with such empirical research, legislative and policy frameworks have also been established that emphasise parental rights in relation to their children's education: the policy message has been strongest and most long-standing in relation to children with special educational needs, as exemplified by the Warnock Report (DES, 1978) and reinforced in both the original and revised versions of the Code of Practice (DfE, 1994b; DfES 2001a). Fragmentation of their learning experiences is particularly problematic for children who struggle with formal education, and therefore it must be of major concern that steps be taken to prevent any breakdown in communication between home and school when children have special needs. Particular sensitivities are, of course, required in those situations where children's difficulties at school are associated with stresses within and upon the family, and it is important to recognise that professionals can, without realising it, add to the pressures that parents experience. Nevertheless, both parents and teachers frequently find that they need to extend their skills and knowledge when children have particular educational needs, and accordingly there is scope for each to provide support for the other in fulfilling their respective roles. In order for such reciprocal support to take place between parents and teachers, however, their communication must be underpinned by mutual trust and respect, which is one of the key qualities required in the relationship if it is to be regarded as a genuine 'partnership'.

Concepts of parent partnership

Notions of parent partnership are complex and indeed problematic in some ways, and while the term is frequently used by professionals and policy makers (although rarely by parents), it is often left undefined. Many of the attempts to characterise partnership and distinguish it from other forms of parental involvement are associated with special education. For example, over twenty years ago, Mittler and Mittler (1982) outlined a number of phases in parent–professional relationships, in which they differentiated between an 'expert' tradition and a 'transplant' model, and contrasted these approaches with more equal forms of partnership. Within the expert tradition, professionals rely almost exclusively on their own professional judgements about appropriate interventions for children with special needs. They may ask parents for information and may also subsequently inform them of what they have decided, but their decisions take little, if any, explicit account of parental views. It might be noted that while this approach is less in evidence than it used to be, it has not gone out of existence. Indeed, there are clear parallels with forms of current practice that have been described in schools that seek to keep parenting and teaching functions separate. For example, citing Swap (1993), Hornby has described as common a form of home–school relationship in which:

> The education of children is carried out at school by teachers. The parents' role is to make sure children get to school on time with the necessary equipment. Parental involvement in

schools is seen as unnecessary and potentially damaging interference in the efficient education of children.

(Hornby, 2000: 18)

In their second example of parent–professional relationships, which they referred to as a transplant model, Mittler and Mittler drew on their colleague Dorothy Jeffree's terminology. She had observed that, as various professionals began to recognise the power of the parental role and the potential resource that parents represented, so they realised that their interventions would be more successful if they were able to draw on the involvement of parents in the role of aides to their interventions. Parents were accordingly enlisted as co-teachers and co-therapists and were instructed in the necessary techniques that they should use with their children: in Jeffree's terms, these techniques were transplanted onto parents in order that they could become involved on the professionals' terms. This approach continues to be a common one, and it should certainly not be assumed that it is restricted to the parents of children with special educational needs. Within mainstream schools, for example, schemes for parental involvement in reading and in other aspects of the curriculum typically follow the transplant approach. An emphasis on the role of parents as co-educators tends to carry with it the idea that parents are in need of professional direction in order to acquire a repertoire of techniques that will give them greater competence. As Hatcher and Leblond (2001) argue, there is a risk here of viewing parents as lacking in skills, rather then recognising their unique contribution as parents.

The Warnock Report (DES, 1978) placed an unequivocally strong emphasis on the need to aim for more of an equal partnership with parents than had hitherto been the case, and since its publication there has been increased attention to what the nature of the ideal relationship between parents and professionals might be. Rather than simply seeing parents as co-educators, the focus has shifted to their role in their own right as parents. This shift can be exemplified by Wolfendale's (1983) emphasis on the parental role as active and central in decision-making processes. Thus Cunningham and Davis (1985), for example, highlighting the extent of the expertise that parents develop in relation to their children, proposed that a 'consumer' model should guide parent–professional relationships. They characterised the approach as one within which parents were encouraged to use their in-depth knowledge and experience of their own children in order to decide upon the services and interventions that were most appropriate for them. These authors were writing before the impact of market forces on education and other public services was felt. Since they put forward their model, there has understandably been a great deal of caution about the type of consumerism that they espoused, not least because of the inequities that arise when so little choice is actually available for the majority of children and their families. Nevertheless, Cunningham and Davis's model has been an important one in the emphasis it placed on the need to listen to parental preferences and views concerning services for their children.

Cunningham and Davis's approach was premised on a recognition of parental rights with respect to information and involvement in decision-making processes. Further developments have tended to stress the importance of appropriate support if parents are to develop the confidence and competence to exercise these rights. For example, Appleton and Minchom's (1991) 'empowerment' model, with its particular emphasis on promoting parental power and control, highlights the need for professionals to tailor their involvement in ways that are responsive to both the strengths and the needs of individual parents and families. More recently, Dale (1996) put forward a model that not only embraces these principles, but also adds a further dimension, based on the acknowledgement that 'dissent may be a major factor in the parent–professional relationship' (Dale, 1996: 15). Accordingly, her framework gives particular attention to the significance of negotiation between parents and professionals in order to achieve joint problem-solving and decision-making.

Although all these models of the parent–professional relationship have been formulated from the perspective of provision for children with special educational needs, their influence has been significant in the development of thinking and policy in mainstream as well as special educational contexts. As a result, although diverse interpretations and uses of the term 'partnership' still remain, some consensus has emerged concerning the core characteristics of a partnership relationship. In the context of parent–teacher communication, the term implies a mutual respect and valuing of what each contributes to children's learning and development; reciprocal acknowledgement of each other's complementary roles and 'equivalent expertise' (Wolfendale, 1983); and genuine two-way communication that allows open sharing of knowledge, information and feelings.

Implementing parent partnership

Although reference to partnership with parents has formed part of policy rhetoric for almost thirty years (since the publication of the Plowden Report, DES, 1967), the reality of the parental experience of involvement with their children's schools may remain far removed from the partnership ideal. The following comments from one mother of an 11-year-old son who experienced learning difficulties at school illustrate some of the barriers to communication with their children's teachers that parents can feel:

> 'As a parent, you've got to get involved . . . You may feel intimidated but you must put your own self to one side, not be intimidated, and say "this is what I feel, I think, I wish for my child", and be ready to say "you're making assumptions – look, you're wrong". Sometimes teachers are so harassed and pressurised and stressed that to say they've got to reach out to parents may be too much. But as a parent you do feel the barriers are there, you feel pressurised to justify yourself a lot – there needs to be a way to bring the barriers down'.
>
> (Beveridge, 1997: 56)

There is no doubt that it takes both time and considerable skills and commitment on the part of teachers if they are to build up constructive partnerships with parents, and it is essential to recognise the barriers that may need to be overcome. Pinkus (2003) believes that many of the problems in parent–professional relationships stem from continuing confusion about the interconnections between consumerism and partnership models. She argues that there has been too much emphasis on the 'soft' qualities that underpin notions of partnership and insufficient attention to the ways in which parent and teacher roles and responsibilities can be defined and operationalised. However, it is within those interpersonal qualities of the relationship that the nature of partnership lies and there cannot be a single blueprint for the way that this operates. Rather, there is a need for flexible responsiveness to individual diversity between parents and also an accommodation to the shifts and changes in the home–school relationship that occur as children progress through their schooling. Dale (1996) has highlighted some of the different levels at which partnership must function: personal, interpersonal, organisational, positional and ideological. A consideration of each of these levels provides a reminder of the ecological framework within which home–school relationships are contextualised, and through doing so, also serves to illuminate the complexities involved.

At the *personal level*, both parents and teachers differ in numerous ways in terms of their beliefs, values, knowledge and understandings related to children's development and learning and to aspects of educational provision. As a result there is variation both in their motivations and confidence for working together as well as in the personal resources that they bring to any partnership relationship. Some parents may feel diffident or unsure about what they might contribute to their children's formal education: others may invest a great deal of emotional effort, energy and determination in order to influence the nature of the provision that is made. Such personal attributes and perspectives have evident implications for the ways in which a partnership functions at the *interpersonal level*. Research by Croll and Moses (1985, 2000) has identified the extent to which teachers may attribute children's learning and behaviour difficulties in school to home-based factors and it is clear that parents are typically well aware of any assumptions of this kind that staff make. There is an evident need to develop professional awareness and understanding of the complex interacting factors that contribute both to children's development and to their particular educational needs. This would not only help to prevent oversimplistic attributions of causes of children's difficulty, but would also provide a better-informed basis from which to work together with their parents to seek possible solutions. The nature of home–school communication is powerfully influenced by the attitudes and strategies that teachers adopt. As discussed in Chapter 6, parents value teachers who demonstrate openness, approachability and genuine care and concern for their children. Mordaunt (2001) has observed that parent–teacher relationships are likely to be tested at times, and therefore the relationship needs to be strong enough to deal with misunderstandings and disagreements. Accordingly, teachers also require the sorts of highly developed communication skills that allow them to engage with parents on potentially delicate topics with accuracy, honesty and sensitivity; to reconcile differing perspectives when these exist; and to negotiate agreed decisions.

On an *organisational level*, structures and processes both at home and at school influence the forms of relationships that parents and teachers can develop. At home, for example, patterns of parental employment often restrict opportunities for liaison with school, and competing family pressures can affect the priority given to particular home–school initiatives. Similarly, the size, organisation, staff roles and responsibilities of primary, secondary and special schools all have an impact on the nature of the home–school contacts that typically take place. Not all parents are familiar with the organisational structures in their children's schools and neither do all teachers have relevant and accurate information about their pupils' home circumstances. However, there is little doubt that the quality of home–school communication will be more positive when parental and teacher expectations are informed by mutual understanding of the demands, opportunities and constraints that operate in each setting. Just as there are limits to the amount of time and energy that parents can dedicate to their involvement with schools, so there are clearly practical limitations on the extent to which schools can be responsive to individual family diversity. Nevertheless, it should also be acknowledged that schools differ significantly in their commitment, whole-school policies and staff development practice regarding partnership, and that very often there is scope to extend the range and flexibility of the approaches that they adopt in their communications with pupils' parents.

The *positional level* identified by Dale (1996) incorporates both role and power positions. Parental and teacher *roles* in children's education, while complementary, are necessarily different. Typically parents have in-depth and intimate knowledge and experience of their children, which is characterised by high emotional involvement and attachment, and by continuity over time and across a varied range of contexts. In contrast, teachers' experience of children's development has a broader perspective and is informed by professional knowledge of teaching and learning. The role that teachers fulfil requires them to balance attention to the individual with the needs of a larger group, and therefore their relationship with individual children is less in-depth and more detached, and is typically time-limited and focused on formal learning within school contexts. An explicit acknowledgement of such differences in parental and teacher roles brings with it a number of implications. The first is that there is a potential source of tension between a parental focus on their own children and teachers' school-wide responsibilities for pupils that may need to be resolved. Second, it is to be expected that as a result of the differing knowledge and experiences associated with their roles, parents and teachers will hold differing, and sometimes discrepant, perspectives on individual children. An acknowledgement of the personal and emotional investment of parents should not lead to an assumption that their views are in some way less rational and carry less weight than those of professionals. If parents and teachers are both to be regarded as deriving 'equivalent expertise' (Wolfendale, 1983) from their roles, then educational decision-making must be based on the negotiation of their differing perspectives. There is, therefore, the need to recognise and respect what Dale (1996) has referred to as the validity of dissent. Linked to this, a further implication arises from a consideration of what it might mean to describe parental and teacher roles in education as complementary. It can be argued that approaches to home–school liaison are too often premised on the assumption that the parental role is to support the school and the school's agenda (Vincent, 2000), and therefore that parental involvement still tends to take place on the school's terms (Dyson and Robson, 1999). Although parents can be regarded as natural teachers of their children, their educational role goes far beyond the support of school-directed activities and tasks. A challenge for teachers who wish to work in partnership is therefore to recognise and value that broader parental contribution through involving parents in dialogue about their children's education on an equal footing.

Any attempt to work with parents in a partnership relationship also has to engage with the *power positions* that are involved. As discussed in Chapter 2, inequities arise from parental involvement policies because some parents are more able than others to take up their rights to involvement in their children's education. However, Mittler (2000) is one of those who has highlighted the imbalance of power even in situations where there is positive and constructive dialogue between parents and teachers: 'Parents and teachers may be friendly, helpful and polite to one another but there is an unavoidable underlying tension that arises from the imbalance of power between them' (p. 151).

Parent–teacher meetings, even those seen by teachers as 'informal', tend to advantage the professionals, who typically set the agenda and convene the meeting on their own 'home territory'. In more formal meetings, such as those required by decision-making procedures in respect of children with special educational needs, there is ample evidence that few parents feel they have equal status and power to that of professionals (e.g. Galloway, 1985; Galloway *et al.*, 1994; Armstrong, 1995; Vincent, 1996). It should be noted, though, that it is not unusual for parents and teachers to have different views concerning the nature of the decision-making that has taken place in a meeting, and who has taken the lead in any decisions reached. Pinkus (2003) provides a useful reminder of the complexities involved by pointing out that, although parents are typically portrayed in research as the 'weaker partners' in the relationship, it is not always experienced in that way by the professionals with whom they are involved. Just like parents, therefore, teachers can themselves feel under a great deal of stress when participating in joint decision-making meetings.

The nature of the power relationships that exist between parents and teachers clearly reflects wider *ideological* frameworks, such as those represented within national governmental policy. In Chapter 2, attention was drawn to some of the inconsistencies in those policy initiatives, which cast parents in the role of individual consumers and also, at the same time, as partners in a collaborative educational endeavour with schools. Vincent (2000) has elaborated on the resulting tensions within the home–school relationship, and in particular highlights the ways in which a policy focus on individualistic forms of parental involvement almost inevitably leads to inequities of power. She argues that, if parents are to have more equal power in their interactions with schools, this requires the development of policy frameworks within which parents can participate more effectively through collective action. There is little doubt that involvement with parent groups can be empowering for the individuals concerned. As Vincent acknowledges, however, such groups can also act to consolidate the advantage of one group of children over another. For this reason, Martin (2000) proposes that a more equitable system would need to ensure that diverse parent interest groups all have a voice in decisions about provision for their children.

This consideration of the many interacting levels that influence the development of home–school relationships highlights the layers of complexity involved in seeking to implement a partnership approach. These complexities are compounded by the recognition that the relationship must take into account not only individual parents and teachers, but also whole-family dynamics and whole-school practices. Further, it can be argued that the principles that underpin parent–teacher partnerships must also be extended to embrace the participation of other professionals as well as the children themselves in educational decision-making processes.

Extending the relationship: including other professionals

Although this book has focused on parent–teacher relationships, these cannot be seen in isolation from wider professional networks, both within and beyond school. For pupils with particular needs, support staff in schools fulfil a range of functions that can include home–school liaison, and beyond school, interdisciplinary involvement is a well-established and fundamental principle of service provision. Recognition of the need for multi-agency collaboration is central, for example, to the Code of Practice for children with special educational needs (DfES, 2001a) and to current government strategy in this area (DfES, 2003b, 2004). For those who are at risk of educational disadvantage, it is identified within national policy initiatives as being essential both for preventing difficulties from occurring where possible, and for responding to the difficulties that do arise.

As outlined in the introductory chapter of this book, where different professionals have a significant role to play in provision for children and their families, Bronfenbrenner's (1977) ecological model provides a clear theoretical explanation of the importance of effective channels for communication and liaison between them. However, there is ample evidence that close collaboration and a coordinated approach between differing professionals is not always easy to achieve (see, for example, Riddell and Tett, 2001). Dessent (1996) and Dyson *et al.* (1998) have highlighted some of the barriers to interdisciplinary working that arise from the differing legislative frameworks and organisational constraints that operate for different professional groups. Further difficulties arise when the services that they work for hold differing priorities, employ differing definitions of child and family needs and are underpinned by differing values and goals. If there is fragmentation of the service that is provided, then professionals can lose sight of 'the whole child', inadvertently contributing to further disadvantage. The involvement of several different agencies also increases the risk that professionals contribute to family stress, for example by the provision of overlapping and confusing, or even conflicting, advice.

Despite the difficulties that can stand in the way of effective inter-professional collaboration, however, there is evidence from the studies undertaken by both Dessent (1996) and Dyson *et al.* (1998) that the commitment of the individuals concerned can make a significant and positive difference to the extent of coordination in the service that children and their families receive. At this interpersonal level, the conditions required for successful inter-professional working are essentially similar to those involved in developing individual partnerships with parents. That is, there is a need for a shared sense of purpose and goals, and a knowledge and understanding of what each has to offer in order to fulfil these. This in turn requires clarity about boundaries and overlaps between each other's roles and responsibilities, and a preparedness for responsive communication based on reciprocal trust and respect for each other's contribution.

It was highlighted earlier in this chapter that any attempt to work in partnership with children's parents must take account of the complexities that arise, not only from interpersonal factors, but also from wider considerations relating to the organisational, positional and ideological levels within which the relationships function. The same is undoubtedly true of inter-professional collaboration. It follows therefore that teachers face considerable challenges if they are to extend their partnerships with parents in ways that include other professionals too. Referring to children with special educational needs, Russell (1992) proposed that parents themselves have a significant facilitative role to play in the process: she argues that because parental perspectives on their children are holistic, they are well placed to integrate the individual concerns of all the professionals who are involved. In a similar vein, Davie (1993) observed that the children themselves can fulfil an integrative function if they are viewed as full participants in the decision-making that takes place.

Extending the relationship: children's participation

Previous chapters have drawn attention to the increasing recognition that children are active contributors to their experiences at home, at school and in other community learning contexts, and that they have the right to express their views and have these taken seriously. Evidence is beginning to accumulate of the developmental benefits for children when they participate in decisions related to service provision, and the government has asserted its commitment to the principle (CYPU, 2000). Nevertheless, pupil participation in decision-making at school is a less well-established notion than that of parent–teacher partnership. This has led some researchers (e.g. Edwards, 2002) to express concerns that an emphasis on parents has distracted attention away from the need to seek out and listen to their children's views, and there is no doubt that there are areas of tension between these two principles. However, it has been argued in this book that children must be viewed as key contributors to the development of constructive home–school liaison. They are the focus for communication and can have a significant influence on the nature of the relationship that is established between their parents and teachers. When they are systematically involved in home–school consultation processes, this offers a potentially powerful opportunity for enhancing their active participation in educational decision-making.

Children have distinctive perspectives on their learning experiences, needs and aspirations and, as a result, their views do not necessarily coincide with those of their parents or their teachers. The bringing together of parent, child and teacher contributions to decision-making is clearly therefore a complex task. Any attempt to address this complexity must take into account the power relationships that exist between and among parents, teachers and children. Accordingly, children's rights must be balanced with parental rights, and those rights must also be set against the responsibilities for children's well-being that are associated with both parental and teacher roles. In addition, there is a need to acknowledge the ways in which cultural and gender variables (e.g. Morrow, 1998) and the presence of special needs (e.g. Read, 2000) are likely to influence parental views concerning appropriate expectations of their children's developing autonomy.

Among teachers, as among parents, it is to be expected that there will be diverse perspectives concerning the priority that should be given to children's views, and for this reason it is important that whole-school policies on pupil participation should be agreed. Such individual variation is not restricted to the adults concerned, however, because children also differ in the extent to which they wish to participate, at least in more formal settings for decision-making, such as consultation and review meetings. Schools therefore need to find forms of involvement with which children feel comfortable, and through which over time they can build up their confidence and skills for further participation. They will be supported in this task if they draw upon the experiences that parents have of their children's decision-making in out-of-school contexts. It is often assumed that professionals will need to induct parents into ways of allowing their children to speak up for themselves. While there are clearly situations where this is required, it is equally clear that in other cases it is parents who take on a mediation role with schools in order to ensure that their children's perspectives are listened to and given due weight (e.g. Ericsson and Larsen, 2002; Beveridge, 2004). Indeed, there is evidence (Kirby *et al.*, 2003) that children are more likely to rate their parents than their teachers as being good at listening to their views. As discussed in Chapter 6, parents and teachers are likely to have the sort of complementary experiences that can form the basis of mutual support. They do, though, also need to respect the distance that children may wish to keep between aspects of their lives at home and at school.

Current policy initiatives require the involvement of both parents and children in decision-making and review processes at school. It is crucial to the attempt to work together in this way that schools develop an agreed vocabulary and framework for communicating about the nature and extent of pupil participation that is aimed for in particular circumstances. For example, Kirby and her colleagues have described a four-level categorisation as follows:

1   children/young people's views are taken into account by adults;
2   children/young people are included in decision-making (together with adults);
3   children/young people share power and responsibility for decision-making with adults;
4   children/young people make autonomous decisions.

(Kirby *et al.*, 2003: 22)

This sort of categorisation, which is not intended to be hierarchical, might usefully form a basis for discussion between teachers, pupils and parents about appropriate levels of participation for different aspects of decision-making.

There is no doubt that the requirement to ensure that both parent and pupil voices are given due weight makes considerable demands on professional skills and sensitivities. For teachers of children with special educational needs, the Code of Practice and associated SEN Toolkit (DfES, 2001a, 2001b) seek to address some of the complex issues involved and offer some starting points for the development of school practice. Although these highlight particular concerns for children with special educational needs, they have a wider whole-school applicability.

Partnership, participation and inclusive educational practice

Throughout this book, the aim has been to locate its central themes of partnership and participation within the context of inclusive education. Following Norwich's (1996) framework, this has involved a consideration of three interrelated perspectives on the development of policy and practice: those that are *common* across all children and families; those that reflect the need to acknowledge *individual* diversity; and those that highlight *exceptional* issues related to special educational needs. It can be argued that the principles of participation and partnership are fundamental to the development of inclusive educational practice. By definition, inclusive education must be concerned with the dual processes of maximising participation and reducing exclusion. This requires the active promotion of positive relationships that seek to ensure that all concerned, and most especially the children and their parents and staff, feel that they are valued participants in a school's learning community.

Over recent years, there has been a growing acknowledgement not only of the importance of active involvement in decision-making processes for children in general, but also of its particular significance for those who are at greatest risk of marginalisation. As a result, pupil participation in decision-making at school has been identified as a core element of strategies for combating educational disadvantage and exclusion (Cox, 2000). It is not only children, though, but also their parents, who may experience marginalisation. For this reason, Mittler (2000) has argued that 'A government committed to inclusion has to tackle the exclusion of so many parents from participation in discussion and decision making about the education of their children' (p. 169). At individual school level, therefore, Mittler's argument offers an explicit reminder that the development of inclusive practice requires strategies for establishing constructive home–school relationships for all pupils. To be effective, these strategies must be both informed by and responsive to the particular issues that can arise for parents of children with special educational needs.

The notion of partnership carries with it a recognition and valuing of the complementary knowledge and understanding of all the participants in the relationship. With respect to inclusion, there is no doubt that children and parents have unique insights and experiences that need to be listened to and taken seriously. For schools that aspire to inclusive educational practice, therefore, a key strategy must be to seek ways of building on the potential resource that the participation of children and their parents represents.

References

Alderson, P. (2000) School students' views on school councils and daily life at school. *Children and Society*, **14**, 121–134.

Alderson, P. (2002) Students' rights in British schools: trust, autonomy, connection and regulation. In R. Edwards (ed.) *Children, Home and School: regulation, autonomy or connection*. London: RoutledgeFalmer.

Allan, J. (1999) *Actively Seeking Inclusion: pupils with special needs in mainstream schools*. London: Falmer Press.

Alldred, P., David, M. and Edwards, R. (2002) Minding the gap: children and young people negotiating relations between home and school. In R. Edwards. (ed.) *Children, Home and School: regulation, autonomy or connection*. London: RoutledgeFalmer.

Appleton, P. L. and Minchom, P. E. (1991) Models of parent partnership and child development centres. *Child: care, health and development*, **17**, 27–38.

Armstrong, D. (1995) *Power and Partnership in Education*. London: Routledge.

Atkin, J. and Bastiani, J. (1986) 'Are they teaching?': an alternative perspective on parents as educators. *Education 3–13*, **14**, 18–22.

Bailey, J. (1998) Australia: inclusion through categorisation? In T. Booth and M. Ainscow (eds) *From Them to Us: an international study of inclusion in education*. London: Routledge.

Ball, M. (1998) *School Inclusion: the school, the family and the community*. York: Joseph Rowntree Foundation.

Barton, L., Oliver, M. and Barnes, C. (2002) Disability: the importance of sociological analysis. In M. Holborn (ed.) *Developments in Sociology: an annual review. Vol. 18*. Ormskirk: Causeway Press.

Bastiani, J. (1992) *Working with Parents: a whole school approach*. Windsor: NFER-Nelson.

Bastiani, J. (ed.) (1997) *Home-School Work in Multicultural Settings*. London: David Fulton.

Bates, I. and Wilson, P. (2003) *Exploring Family Interaction around Young People's Lives and Learning: possibilities and limitations of cultural capital.* Paper presented at University of Leeds Lifelong Learning Institute Seminar 'Families as Sites of Learning', June 18, 2003.

Bearne, E. (2002) A good listening to: Year 3 pupils talk about learning. *Support for Learning*, **17**, 3, 122–127.

Beresford, B. (1995) *Expert Opinions: a national survey of parents caring for a severely disabled child.* Bristol: Policy Press.

Beresford, B. (1997) *Personal Accounts: involving disabled children in research.* London: The Stationery Office.

Berrueta-Clement, J. R., Schweinhart, L. J., Barnett, W. S., Epstein, A. S. and Weikart, D. P. (1984) *Changed Lives: the effects of the Perry preschool program on youths through age 19.* Ypsilanti: High Scope Press.

Beveridge, S. (1989) Parents as teachers of children with special educational needs. In D. Sugden (ed.) *Cognitive Approaches in Special Education.* Lewes: Falmer Press.

Beveridge, S. (1997) Implementing partnership with parents in schools. In S. Wolfendale (ed.) *Working with Parents of SEN Children after the Code of Practice.* London: David Fulton.

Beveridge, S. (2004) Pupil participation and the home–school relationship. *European Journal of Special Needs Education*, **19**, 1, 3–16.

Blunkett, D. (1997) Editorial. *British Journal of Special Education*, **24**, 4, 150–151.

Booth, T. (1998) The poverty of special education: theories to the rescue? In C. Clark, A. Dyson and A. Millward (eds) *Theorising Special Education.* London: Routledge.

Brannen, J. (1996) Discourses of adolescence: young people's independence and autonomy within families. In J. Brannen and M. O'Brien (eds) *Children in Families: research and policy.* London: Falmer Press.

Brannen, J. and O'Brien, M. (eds) (1996) *Children in Families: research and policy.* London: Falmer Press.

Brannen, J., Heptinstall, E. and Bhopal, K. (2000) *Connecting Children: care and family life in later childhood.* London: RoutledgeFalmer.

Bronfenbrenner, U. (1976) Is early intervention effective? Facts and principles of early intervention: a summary. In A. M. and A. D. B. Clarke (eds) *Early Experience: myth and evidence.* London: Open Books.

Bronfenbrenner, U. (1977) Towards an ecology of human development. *American Psychologist*, **32**, 513–531.

Bronfenbrenner, U. (1979) *The Ecology of Human Development.* Cambridge, Mass. and London: Harvard University Press.

Broomhead, C. (1998) Planned transition from education to employment for young people with severe learning difficulties. In C. Tilstone, L. Florian and R. Rose (eds) *Promoting Inclusive Practice.* London: Routledge.

Brown, C. (1999) Parent voices on advocacy, education, disability and justice. In K. Ballard (ed.) *Inclusive Education: international voices on disability and justice.* London: Falmer Press.

Carpenter, B. and Herbert, E. (1997) Fathers: are we meeting their needs? In B. Carpenter (ed.) *Families in Context: emerging trends in family support and early intervention.* London: David Fulton.

Carpenter, S. and Carpenter, B. (1997) Working with families. In B. Carpenter (ed.) *Families in Context: emerging trends in family support and early intervention.* London: David Fulton.

Centre for Studies in Inclusive Education (2000) *Index for Inclusion: developing learning and participation in schools.* Bristol: CSIE and London: DfEE.

Chamba, R., Ahmad, W., Hirst, M., Lawton, D. and Beresford, B. (1999) *On the Edge: minority ethnic families caring for a severely disabled child.* Bristol: Policy Press.

Chazan, M. (2000) Social disadvantage and disruptive behaviour in school. In T. Cox (ed.) *Combating Educational Disadvantage: meeting the needs of vulnerable children.* London: Falmer Press.

Clarke, L. (1996) Demographic change and the family situation of children. In J. Brannen and M. O'Brien (eds) *Children in Families: research and policy.* London: Falmer Press.

Coleman, P. (1998) *Parent, Student and Teacher Collaboration: the power of three.* London: Paul Chapman.

Coulling, N. (2000) Definitions of successful education for the 'looked after' child: a multiagency perspective. *Support for Learning,* **15**, 1, 30–35.

Cox, T. (2000) Pupils' perspectives on their education. In T. Cox (ed.) *Combating Educational Disadvantage: meeting the needs of vulnerable children.* London: Falmer Press.

Croll, P. (2002) Social deprivation, school-level achievement and special educational needs. *Educational Research,* **44**, 43–53.

Croll, P. and Moses, D. (1985) *One in Five: the assessment and incidence of special educational needs.* London: Routledge & Kegan Paul.

Croll, P. and Moses, D. (2000) *Special Needs in the Primary School.* London: Cassell.

Crowther, D., Cummings, C., Dyson, A. and Millward, A. (2003) How schools can contribute to area regeneration. *Joseph Rowntree Findings 983,* www.jrf.org.uk/knowledge/findings/housing/983.asp (accessed 2 October 2003).

Crozier, G. (2000) *Parents and Schools: partners or protagonists?* Stoke on Trent: Trentham Books.

Cunningham, C. C. and Davis, H. (1985) *Working with Parents: frameworks for collaboration.* Milton Keynes: Open University Press.

CYPU (2000) *Tomorrow's Future: building a strategy for children and young people.* London: Children and Young People's Unit.

Dale, N. (1996) *Working with Families of Children with Special Needs*. London: Routledge.

Davie, R. (1993) Interdisciplinary perspectives on assessment. In S. Wolfendale (ed.) *Assessing Special Educational Needs*. London: Cassell.

Davie, R. (1996) Raising the achievements of pupils with special educational needs. *Support for Learning*, **11**, 2, 51–56.

Davie, R. (2000) Foreword. In T. Cox (ed.) *Combating Educational Disadvantage: meeting the needs of vulnerable children*. London: Falmer Press.

Dee, L. (2000) Transition: how can it be improved. In H. Daniels (ed.) *Special Education Re-formed: beyond rhetoric*. London: Falmer Press.

Dee, L. (2002) 'Am I the same?' Decision-making processes during the transition from school. *Journal of Research in Special Educational Needs*, **2**, 2.

DES (1967) *Children and their Primary Schools* (The Plowden Report). London: HMSO.

DES (1978) *Special Educational Needs* (The Warnock Report), Cmnd 7212. London: HMSO.

DES (1989) *Discipline in Schools* (The Elton Report). London: HMSO.

Dessent, T. (1996) *Options for Partnership between Health, Education and Social Services*. Policy Options for Special Educational Needs in the 1990s, Seminar Paper 6. Tamworth: NASEN.

DfE (1994a) *Our Children's Education: the Updated Parent's Charter*. London: HMSO.

DfE (1994b) *Code of Practice on the Identification and Assessment of Special Educational Needs*. London: DfE.

DfEE (1997a) *Excellence for all Children: meeting special educational needs*. London: The Stationery Office.

DfEE (1997b) *The SENCO Guide*. London: DfEE.

DfEE (1998) *Meeting Special Educational Needs: a programme of action*. London: DfEE.

DfEE (2000) *Guidance on the Education of Children and Young People in Public Care*. London: DfEE.

DfES (2001a) *Special Educational Needs Code of Practice*. London: DfES.

DfES (2001b) *SEN Toolkit*. London: DfES.

DfES (2003a) *Data Collection by Type of Special Educational Need*. Annersley, Nottinghamshire: DfES Publications.

DfES (2003b) *Every Child Matters*. London: The Stationery Office.

DfES (2004) *Removing Barriers to Achievement – the Government's Strategy for Special Educational Needs*. London: DfES.

Diniz, F. A. (1997) Working with families in a multi-ethnic European context: implications for services. In B. Carpenter (ed.) *Families in Context: emerging trends in family support and early intervention*. London: David Fulton.

Dockrell, J. (1997) Children's developing value systems. In G. Lindsay and D. Thompson (eds) *Values into Practice in Special Education*. London: David Fulton.

Dowling, J. and Pound, A. (1994) Joint interventions with teachers, children and parents in the school setting. In E. Dowling and E. Osborne (eds) *The Family and the School: a joint systems approach to problems with children*. London: Routledge.

Dunn, J. (1984) *Sisters and Brothers*. London: Fontana.

Dunn, J. (1998) Young children's understanding of other people: evidence from observations within the family. In M. Woodhead, D. Faulkner and K. Littleton (eds) *Cultural Worlds of Early Childhood*. London: Routledge.

Dyson, A. (1997) Social and educational disadvantage: reconnecting special needs education. *British Journal of Special Education*, **24**, 4, 152–157.

Dyson, A. and Robson, E. (1999) *School, Family, Community: mapping school inclusion in the UK*. Leicester: Youth Work Press for the Joseph Rowntree Foundation.

Dyson, A., Howes, A. and Roberts, B. (2003) A systematic review of the effectiveness of school-level actions for promoting participation by all students. In *Research Evidence in Education Library*. London: EPPI-Centre, Social Science Research Unit, Institute of Education.

Dyson, A., Lin, M. and Millward, A. (1998) *Effective Communication between Schools, LEAs and the Health and Social Services in the Field of Special Needs*. Research Report No 60. Nottingham: DfEE Publications.

Edwards, R. (2002) Introduction: conceptualising relationships between home and school in children's lives. In R. Edwards (ed.) *Children, Home and School: regulation, autonomy or connection*. London: Routledge-Falmer.

Einzig, H. (1999) Review of the field: current trends, concepts and issues. In S. Wolfendale and H. Einzig (eds) *Parenting Education and Support: new opportunities*. London: David Fulton.

Elliott, J. and Place, M. (1998) *Children in Difficulty: a guide to understanding and helping*. London: Routledge.

Ericsson, K. and Larsen, G. (2002) Adults as resources and adults as burdens: the strategies of children in the age of school-home collaboration. In R. Edwards (ed.) *Children, Home and School: regulation, autonomy or connection*. London: RoutledgeFalmer.

Evans, J. and Vincent, C. (1997) Parental choice and special education. In R. Glatter, P. A. Woods and C. Bagley (eds) *Choice and Diversity in Schooling: perspectives and prospects*. London: Routledge.

Evans, P. (2000) Evidence-based practice: how will we know what works? An international perspective. In H. Daniels (ed.) *Special Education Reformed: beyond rhetoric*. London: Falmer Press.

Florian, L. (1998) Inclusive practice: what, why and how? In C. Tilstone, L. Florian and R. Rose (eds) *Promoting Inclusive Practice*. London: Routledge.

Fraser, H. and Honeyford, G. (2000) *Children, Parents and Teachers enjoying Numeracy*. London: David Fulton.

Freeman, M. (2000) The future of children's rights. *Children and Society*, **14**, 277–293.

Friel, J. (1997) *Children with Special Needs: assessment, law and practice: caught in the act*, 4th edition. London: Jessica Kingsley.

Galloway, D. (1985) *Schools, Pupils and Special Educational Needs*. London: Croom Helm.

Galloway, D., Armstrong, D. and Tomlinson, S. (1994) *The Assessment of Special Educational Needs: whose problem?* London: Longman.

Gartner, A. and Lipsky, D. K. (1999) Disability, human rights and education: the United States. In F. Armstrong and L. Barton (eds) *Disability, Human Rights and Education: cross-cultural perspectives*. Buckingham: Open University Press.

Gersch, I. S. with Cope, T., Pratt, G., Sassienie, G., M'Gadzah, S. H., Saraon, S., Sutoris, M. and Townley, D. (2000) Combating unequal access to education: the work of a Local Education Authority Educational Psychology Service. In T. Cox (ed.) *Combating Educational Disadvantage: meeting the needs of vulnerable children*. London: Falmer Press.

Glass, N. (1999) Sure Start: the development of an early intervention programme for young children in the United Kingdom. *Children and Society*, **13**, 257–264.

Goodnow, J. and Burns, A. (1985) *Home and School: a child's eye view*. Sydney: Allen and Unwin.

Grant, C. and Williams, L. J. (2000) The social, economic and political climate in the United States and the education of people of colour. In T. Cox (ed.) *Combating Educational Disadvantage: meeting the needs of vulnerable children*. London: Falmer Press.

Gregory, E. (2000) Recognising differences: reinterpreting family involvement in early literacy. In T. Cox (ed.) *Combating Educational Disadvantage: meeting the needs of vulnerable children*. London: Falmer Press.

Grimshaw, R. and McGuire, C. (1998) *Evaluating Parenting Programmes: a study of stakeholders' views*. London: National Children's Bureau.

Gross, J. (1996) The weight of the evidence: parental advocacy and resource allocation to children with statements of special educational need. *Support for Learning*, **11**, 1, 3–8.

Hannon, P. (1995) *Literacy, Home and School: research and practice in teaching literacy with parents*. London: Falmer.

Hart, S. (1996) *Beyond Special Needs*. London: Paul Chapman.

Hart, S. (1998) Paperwork or practice? Shifting the emphasis of the Code towards teaching, learning and inclusion. *Support for Learning*, **13**, 2, 76–81.

Hatcher, R. and Leblond, D. (2001) Educational Action Zones and Zones d'Education Prioritaires. In S. Riddell and L. Tett (eds) *Education, Social Justice and Inter-Agency Working: joined up or fractured policy?* London: Routledge.

Henricson, C. (2003) Resolving the tensions in parenting policy. *JRF Findings 333*, www.jrf.org.uk/knowledge/findings/socialpolicy/333.asp (accessed 14 April 2003).

Hewison, J. (1988) The long term effectiveness of parental involvement in reading: a follow-up to the Haringey Reading Project. *British Journal of Eduational Psychology*, **58**, 184–190.

Hewison, J. and Tizard, J. (1980) Parental involvement and reading attainment. *British Journal of Educational Psychology*, **50**, 209–215.

Hinton, S. (1999) Support for parents at significant times of transition. In S. Wolfendale and H. Einzig (eds) *Parenting Education and Support: new opportunities*. London: David Fulton.

Home Education UK (2003) *Home Education UK*. www.home-education. org.uk (accessed 23 February 2004).

Home Office (1998) *Supporting Families: a consultation paper*. London: The Stationery Office.

Hornby, G. (1994) *Counselling in Child Disability: skills for working with parents*. London: Chapman and Hall.

Hornby, G. (2000) *Improving Parental Involvement*. London: Continuum.

Hornby, G., Davis, G. and Taylor, G. (1995) *The Special Educational Needs Coordinator's Handbook*. London: Routledge.

Hughes, N. and Carpenter, B. (1991) Annual reviews: an active partnership. In R. Ashdown, B. Carpenter and K. Bovair (eds) *The Curriculum Challenge*. London: Falmer Press.

Jack, G. and Jordan, B. (1999) Social capital and child welfare. *Children and Society*, **13**, 242–256.

James, A., Jenks, C. and Prout, A. (1999) *Theorising Childhood*. London: Polity Press.

Jelly, M., Fuller, A. and Byers, R. (2000) *Involving Pupils in Practice: promoting partnerships with pupils with special educational needs*. London: David Fulton.

Jowett, S., Baginsky, M. and McNeill, M. M. (1991) *Building Bridges: parental involvement in schools*. Windsor: NFER-Nelson.

Kasama, H. and Tett, L. (2001) Involving parents in their children's education in Japan and Scotland: contrasts in policy and practice. In S. Riddell and L. Tett (eds) *Education, Social Justice and Inter-Agency Working: joined-up or fractured policy?* London: Routledge.

Kirby, P., Lanyon, C., Cronin, K. and Sinclair, R. (2003) *Building a Culture of Participation*. London: DfES.

Lazar, I. (1985) On bending twigs and planting acorns: some implications of recent research. *ACPP Newsletter*, **7**, 1, 28–32.

Lazar, I. and Darlington, R. (1983) Lasting effects of early education. *Monographs of the Society for Research in Child Development, Serial No 195*, Vol. 47, Nos 2–3.

McGurk, H. and Soriano, G. (1998) Families and social development: the 21st century. In A. Campbell and S. Muncer (eds) *The Social Child*. Hove: Psychology Press.

Martin, J. (2000) Parents' Organizations: single interest or common good? In H. Daniels (ed.) *Special Education Re-formed: beyond rhetoric*. London: Falmer Press.

Mayall, B. (2001) Understanding childhoods: a London study. In L. Alanen and B. Mayall (eds) *Conceptualising Adult–Child Relations*. London: RoutledgeFalmer.

Meadows, S. (1996) *Parenting Behaviour and Children's Cognitive Development*. Hove: Psychology Press.

Meighan, R. (ed.) (1992) *Learning from Home-based Education*. Ticknall: Education Now Publishing Cooperative.

Meighan, R. (1997) *The Next Learning System: and why home-schoolers are trailblazers*. Nottingham: Educational Heretics Press.

Merttens, R. and Vass, J. (eds) (1993) *Partnerships in Maths: parents and schools*. Lewes: Falmer Press.

Meyer, D. and Vadasy, P. (1997) Meeting the unique concerns of brothers and sisters of children with special needs. In B. Carpenter (ed.) *Families in Context: emerging trends in family support and early intervention*. London: David Fulton.

Miller, A. (2003) *Teachers, Parents and Classroom Behaviour: a psychosocial approach*. Maidenhead: Open University Press.

Mitchell, D. and Brown, R. I. (eds) (1991) *Early Intervention Studies for Young Children with Special Needs*. London: Chapman and Hall.

Mittler, P. (2000) *Working towards Inclusive Education: social contexts*. London: David Fulton.

Mittler, P. and Mittler, H. (1982) *Partnership with Parents*. Stratford-upon-Avon: NCSE.

Mize, J., Russell, A. and Pettit, G. S. (1998) Further explorations of family–peer connections: the role of parenting style in children's development of social competence. In P. T. Slee and K. Rigby (eds) *Children's Peer Relations*. London: Routledge.

Montandon, C. (2001) The negotiation of influence: children's experience of parental educational practices in Geneva. In L. Alanen and B. Mayall (eds) *Conceptualising Adult–Child Relations*. London: RoutledgeFalmer.

Mordaunt, E. (2001) The nature of special educational needs partnerships. In S. Riddell and L. Tett (eds) *Education, Social Justice and Inter-Agency Working: joined-up or fractured policy?* London: Routledge.

Morgan, A. and Piccos, J. (1997) Working with parents to manage children's behaviour. In D. Tattum and G. Herbert (eds) *Bullying: home, school and community.* London: David Fulton.

Morrow, V. (1998) *Understanding Families: children's perspectives.* London: National Children's Bureau.

NESS Research Team (2004) The national evaluation of Sure Start local programmes in England. *Child and Adolescent Mental Health*, **9**, 1, 2–8.

Norwich, B. (1996) Special needs education or education for all: connective specialisation and ideological impurity. *British Journal of Special Education*, **23**, 3, 100–104.

Norwich, B. (1998) *The Future of SEN Policy and Practice after the White and Green Papers.* Paper presented at the Centre for Policy Studies in Education Seminar, University of Leeds, 4 June 1998.

Norwich, B. (2000) Inclusion in education: from concepts, values and critique to practice. In H. Daniels (ed.) *Special Education Re-formed: beyond rhetoric.* London: Falmer Press.

OFSTED (2001) *Evaluating Educational Inclusion: guidance for inspectors and schools.* London: OFSTED.

Palmer, G., North, J., Carr, J. and Kenway, P. (2003) *Monitoring Poverty and Social Exclusion 2003.* York: Joseph Rowntree Foundation.

Parke, R. D., Neville, B., Burks, V. M., Boyum, L. A. and Carson, J. L. (1994) Family–peer relationships: a tripartite model. In R. D. Parke and S. G. Kellam (eds) *Exploring Family Relationships with Other Social Contexts.* Hillsdale, NJ: Lawrence Erlbaum Associates.

de Pear, S. (1997) Excluded pupils' views of their educational needs and experiences. *Support for Learning*, **12**, 19–22.

Pearson, S. (2000) The relationship between school culture and IEPs. *British Journal of Special Education*, **27**, 3, 145–149.

Pellegrini, A. and Galda, L. (1998) *The Development of School-Based Literacy.* London: Routledge.

Pinkus, S. (2003) All talk and no action: transforming the rhetoric of parent–professional partnership into practice. *Journal of Research in Special Educational Needs*, **3**, 2, 115–121.

Power, S. (2001) 'Joined-up thinking?' Inter-agency partnerships in Education Action Zones. In S. Riddell and L. Tett (eds) *Education, Social Justice and Inter-Agency Working: joined-up or fractured policy?* London: Routledge.

Pugh, G., De'Ath, E. and Smith, C. (1994) *Confident Parents, Confident Children.* London: National Children's Bureau.

Punch, S. (2001) Negotiating autonomy: childhoods in rural Bolivia. In L. Alanen and B. Mayall (eds) *Conceptualising Adult–Child Relations*. London: RoutledgeFalmer.

Read, J. (2000) *Disability, the Family and Society: listening to mothers*. Buckingham: Open University Press.

Reynolds, D. (1995) Using school effectiveness knowledge for children with special needs – the problems and possibilities. In A. Clark, A. Dyson and A. Millward (eds) *Towards Inclusive Schools?* London: David Fulton.

Riddell, S. and Tett, L. (eds) (2001) *Education, Social Justice and Inter-Agency Working: joined-up or fractured policy?* London: Routledge.

Roaf, C. (2002) Editorial: Children and young people: advocacy and empowerment. *Support for Learning*, **17**, 3, 102–103.

Roche, J. (1996) The politics of children's rights. In J. Brannen and M. O'Brien (eds) *Children in Families: research and policy*. London: Falmer Press.

Rose, R. (1998) Including pupils: developing a partnership in learning. In C. Tilstone, L. Florian and R. Rose (eds) *Promoting Inclusive Practice*. London: Routledge.

Rose, R., McNamara, S. and O'Neil, J. (1996) Promoting the greater involvement of pupils with special needs in the management of their own assessment and learning processes. *British Journal of Special Education*, **23**, 4, 166–171.

Russell, F. (2003) The expectations of parents of disabled children. *British Journal of Special Education*, **30**, 3, 144–149.

Russell, P. (1991) Access to the National Curriculum for parents. In R. Ashdown, B. Carpenter and K. Bovair (eds) *The Curriculum Challenge*. London: Falmer Press.

Russell, P. (1992) Boundary issues: multidisciplinary working in new contexts – implications for educational psychology practice. In S. Wolfendale, T. Bryans, M. Fox, A. Labram and A. Sigston (eds) *The Profession and Practice of Educational Psychology*. London: Cassell.

Russell, P. (1997) Parents as partners: some early impressions of the impact of the Code of Practice. In S. Wolfendale (ed.) *Working with Parents of SEN Children after the Code of Practice*. London: David Fulton.

Sambrook, T. and Gray, P. (2002) Recognising and working with parents' emotions. In P. Gray (ed.) *Working with Emotions*. London: Routledge-Falmer.

Sandow, S., Stafford, D. and Stafford, P. (1987) *An Agreed Understanding? Parent–professional communication and the 1981 Education Act*. Windsor: NFER-Nelson.

Simmons, K. (2000) Parents, legislation and inclusion. In H. Daniels (ed.) *Special Education Re-formed: beyond rhetoric*. London: Falmer Press.

Swap, S. M. (1993) *Developing Home-School Partnerships*. New York: Teachers College Press.

Sylva, K. (2000) Early childhood education to ensure a 'fair start' for all. In T. Cox (ed.) *Combating Educational Disadvantage: meeting the needs of vulnerable children*. London: Falmer Press.

Sylva, K., Melhuish, E., Sammons, P., Siraj-Blatchford, U., Taggart, B. and Elliot, K. (2003) *The Effective Provision of Pre-school Education (EPPE) Project: findings from the pre-school period. Summary of findings*. Institute of Education: London.

Thomas, G., Walker, D. and Webb, J. (1998) *The Making of the Inclusive School*. London: Routledge.

Tizard, B. and Hughes, M. (1984) *Young Children Learning*. London: Fontana.

Tizard, J., Schofield, W. N. and Hewison, J. (1982) Collaboration between teachers and parents in assisting children's reading. *British Journal of Educational Psychology*, **52**, 1–15.

Tizard, B., Blatchford, P., Burke, J., Farquhar, C. and Plewis, I. (1988) *Young Children at School in the Inner City*. London: Lawrence Erlbaum.

Tomlinson, S. (2000) Ethnic minorities and education: new disadvantages. In T. Cox (ed.) *Combating Educational Disadvantage: meeting the needs of vulnerable children*. London: Falmer Press.

Topping, K. (1998) *The Paired Science Handbook: parental involvement and peer tutoring in science*. London: David Fulton.

Topping, K. and Wolfendale, S. (eds) (1985) *Parental Involvement in Children's Reading*. London: Croom Helm.

Treseder, P. (1997) *Empowering Children and Young People: involvement in decision-making*. London: Save the Children.

United Nations (1989) *Convention on the Rights of the Child*. New York: United Nations.

Vaughan, M. (1989) Parents, children and the legal framework. In C. Roaf and H. Bines (eds) *Needs, Rights and Opportunities: developing approaches to special education*. Lewes: Falmer Press.

Vincent, C. (1996) *Parents and Teachers: power and participation*. London: Falmer Press.

Vincent, C. (2000) *Including Parents? education, citizenship and parental agency*. Buckingham: Open University Press.

Watt, J. (1989) Community education and parental involvement: a partnership in need of a theory. In F. Macleod (ed.) *Parents and Schools: the contemporary challenge*. Lewes: Falmer Press.

Weare, K. (2000) *Promoting Mental, Emotional and Social Health: a whole school approach*. London: Routledge.

Wedell, K. (1995) Making inclusive education ordinary: a national perspective. *British Journal of Special Education*, **22**, 3, 100–104.

Wells, G. (1983) Talking with children: the complementary roles of parents and teachers. In M. Donaldson, R. Grieve and C. Pratt (eds) *Early Childhood Development and Education*. Oxford: Blackwell.

White, M. (1997) A review of the influence and effects of Portage. In S. Wolfendale (ed.) *Working with Parents of SEN Children after the Code of Practice.* London: David Fulton.

Wolfendale, S. (1983) *Parental Participation in the Education and Development of Children.* London: Gordon and Breach.

Wolfendale, S. (1986) Involving parents in behaviour management: a whole school approach. *Support for Learning,* **1**, 4, 32–38.

Wolfendale, S. (1987) *Primary Schools and Special Needs: policy, planning and provision.* London: Cassell.

Wolfendale, S. (1988) *The Parental Contribution to Assessment.* Stratford-upon-Avon: NCSE.

Wolfendale, S. (1992) *Empowering Parents and Teachers.* London: Cassell.

Wolfendale, S. (ed.) (1993) *Assessing Special Educational Needs.* London: Cassell.

Wolfendale, S. and Bastiani, J. (eds) (2000) *The Contribution of Parents to School Effectiveness.* London: David Fulton.

Wolfendale, S. and Cook, G. (1997) *Evaluation of Special Educational Needs Parent Partnership Schemes.* Research Report 34. London: DfEE.

Wolfendale, S. and Einzig, H. (eds) (1999) *Parenting Education and Support: new opportunities.* London: David Fulton.

Wolfendale, S. and Topping, K. (eds) (1995) *Family Involvement in Literacy.* London: Cassell.

Wragg, T. (1989) Parent power. In F. Macleod (ed.) *Parents and Schools: the contemporary challenge.* Lewes: Falmer Press.

Wright, C., Weekes, D. and McGlaughlin, A. (2000) *'Race', Class and Gender in Exclusion from School.* London: Falmer Press.

Wyness, M. G. (2000) *Contesting Childhood.* London: Falmer Press.

Index